Also by Diana Shaw

VEGETARIAN ENTERTAINING

SWEET BASIL, GARLIC, TOMATOES, AND CHIVES

GRILLING FROM THE GARDEN

Vegetarian Dishes for the
Outdoor Cook

Diana Shaw

Harmony Books
New York

Published by Harmony Books, a division of Crown Publishers, Inc., 201 East 50th Street,
New York, New York 10022. Member of the Crown Publishing Group.
Random House Inc. New York, Toronto, London, Sydney, Auckland
Harmony and colophon are trademarks of Crown Publishers, Inc.

Manufactured in the United States of America
Book design by Linda Kocur

Library of Congress Cataloging-in-Publication Data
Shaw, Diana
Grilling from the garden : vegetarian dishes for the outdoor cook
Diana Shaw. — 1st ed.
p. cm
Includes index.
1. Barbecue cookery. 2. Vegetarian cookery. I. Title
TX840.B3S47   1993
641.5' 784—dc20   92-22898
CIP

ISBN 0-517-88042-3
10 9 8 7 6 5 4 3 2 1
First Edition

With love, laughs, and lavosh to
Lisa Flaherty Shaw
My brother's keeper
and the mother of my niece

CONTENTS

7

Good things come to those who wait.

—Anthony Shaw (my father) grilling, Summer 1963

INTRODUCTION

I love summer. I even lived in Los Angeles for a while, thinking it would be great to have summer all year long. ❧ It was great at first—great not to have to worry about losing my gloves or losing my fingers if I did. It was nice to go sailing and cycling in February and to get that wholesome sun-burnished look just bringing the groceries in from the car. I did not miss the snow, less the sleet and slush. ❧ But what is not longed for isn't cherished. ❧ I missed *missing* summers. I missed dreaming day after gray barren day of what I would do, how I would live when the cracked frozen earth went through its annual miracle of refinement and sent up soft green shoots toward the sun. ❧ Naturally, my dreams of summer had much to do with food. In other words, they concerned grilling. But since I'd decided to stop eating meat, I had trouble imagining what to put on the grill. Eggplant, mushrooms, peppers, tomatoes, and onions sizzled away on my phantom skewers until I was sick of them. Even in reverie, grilling without meat was immensely monotonous. ❧ I had a thought: For centuries our ancestors cooked vegetables on an open hearth, using rudimentary methods. To broaden my grilling repertoire, I began fixing contemporary vegetarian meals in this primitive manner.

I also adapted recipes from cuisines with the dual traditions of grill and vegetable cookery. Throughout much of Africa, Mexico, the Caribbean, and South America, as well as the Middle and Far East, foods of all kinds are prepared over an open flame. Vegetables and grains figure prominently, if not exclusively in many dishes. *Grilling from the Garden* presents my versions of such dishes, which I hope you will enjoy.

GETTING STARTED

With all the fancy grill gadgets around today, and many zealots offering specific, authoritative advice concerning their use, I feel a bit silly giving the simple grilling instructions that follow. But every time I think about approaching grilling as if it were a skill-intensive technique akin to bread baking, say, or even potato mashing, I come back to the fact that it was the Cro-Magnon's cooking method of choice, calling for as much culinary acumen as you'd expect in that case. Grilling is easy, and to complicate it by suggesting you learn a lot of fancy tricks would, I think, spoil the fun.

CHOOSING A GRILL

Don't let the snazzier grills on the market today persuade you that you need something more sophisticated than you might have needed five or ten years back. You're bound to find a perfectly adequate grill at any well-stocked hardware store.

13

If you really want a fancy state-of-the-art model, and you can make sense of the instruction book and handle the assembly kit, you'll find it wherever expensive cooking gear is sold.

I tested all of the recipes in this book on Mr. Grill, a vertical grill available from Hammacher Schlemmer (see the appendix for the toll-free number). The grill is the size of a standard hibachi, but doubles the cooking surface by allowing you to grill on both sides of the heat source. The heat source is a wire cage that stands upright in the center of the grill and can be filled with various fuels. For the purpose of testing each recipe in this book, I used pure mesquite. There are brackets on each side of the cage that hold removable mesh grilling screens, which, in turn, hold the food.

I've found that the most important feature to consider when you're choosing a grill is the surface space. The more room you have, the more food you can cook at once, and the less you have to worry that the heat will die before everything's done.

Another important feature is an adjustable grilling surface with a range of six inches that can be raised and lowered as needed. This will help you control how quickly and thoroughly your food is cooked.

Most grills come with a cover. While hibachis rarely include covers, there's a great hybrid out now, called a tabletop grill, which is essentially a hibachi with a cover. When cooking for up to four people, I would choose this grill. For more, I'd opt for the conventional backyard model—the kind you may have rusting in your garage at this very moment.

STARTING THE FIRE

Now that safe, clean, solid synthetic fire starters are widely available, I don't use any other method. The waxy, corklike substance—sold under various commercial names alongside charcoal wherever charcoal is sold—comes in square sheets or rectangular blocks and costs only pennies per use. It allows you to use 100 percent mesquite (the most flavorful fuel for the purposes of the recipes in this book) without dousing it with lighter fluid and risking those notorious flare-ups and fumes.

Simply fill the basin of your grill or hibachi with mesquite and/or coals to a depth of three inches or so. Tear the fire starter into tiny wads and scatter it among the coals. Light the wads, and you'll have a good blaze going within a minute.

Because it takes so long for the coals to reach an adequate cooking temperature, start the fire at least forty minutes before you plan to cook. And keep in mind that grilling works backward in that the grill will reach high first and then, as the coals cool, it will change to medium, then low.

Vegetables taste best grilled over pure mesquite. You may have heard that tossing herbs into the fire adds flavor to the food, but I've found this far less effective than seasoning the food itself. Flavored wood chips, such as honey wood chips, soaked according to package directions and mixed with mesquite, can have a nice effect, but only on vegetables that spend five minutes or more on the grill, such as mushrooms.

Testing the Heat

Start testing only after flames and smoke have subsided altogether, and a fine gray ash covers the coals. Then hold your hand five inches above the coals.

If you can stand it for two to three seconds, your heat is High, the temperature for most of the recipes in this book.

If you can stand it for four to six seconds, your heat is Medium, the temperature for most dishes involving bread or grains.

If you can stand it for seven to nine seconds, your heat is Low, and suitable for marshmallows.

It takes some practice to figure out how long to cook foods on the grill, especially vegetables that have been precooked a bit, as many recipes will suggest. The cooking times

I've given are approximate and may have more to do with the idiosyncrasies of my grill and my own preferences than with kitchen science. Eventually you'll feel confident enough to trust your judgment about when dinner's ready.

Cooking Times

I've decided to devote this book to charcoal flame grilling, so the cooking times given are for conventional grills. If you'd like to try the recipes on a gas, electric, or stove-top grill, you can use the same ingredients in the same proportions, but you may have to adjust the cooking time according to the amount of heat your appliance generates.

ACCESSORIES

Some of my recipes call for "special equipment," but most of what's needed is fairly common; I just want to call your attention to it so you'll have it handy when the time comes to put it to use. Here's what you can expect to find in this category:

Fine-mesh grill grate. This is a device for grilling foods that might otherwise fall between the cracks. The grilling surface can be used over, or in place of, the grate on your grill. You'll need this only if the grate on your grill is wider than one-eighth inch. Any well-supplied hardware store should have one.

A long-handled wire-mesh grill screen. This is a flat caged device that opens on a hinge. You place food inside, clamp it shut, then either hold it above the fire (if you are browning bread for a sandwich, for example) or lay it on the grill to ensure even cooking.

Wooden skewers for kebabs. These are very handy to have around, but be sure to always soak them in water for thirty minutes before using them, or they might ignite.

A soft-bristled pastry brush. An indispensable tool for brushing the grill with oil and for basting the vegetables.

Some other tools that will come in handy are the following:

Sharp paring knife for testing doneness

Thin butter knife for spreading filling into narrow cavities

Aluminum foil for wrapping certain vegetables, such as corn on the cob or russet potatoes, and for improvising a cover if your grill has none

Tongs and a large flat metal spatula for removing food from the grill

Microwave oven for blanching vegetables

SAFETY INFORMATION

CHOOSE YOUR SITE WITH CARE

Make sure the site is clear of flammable objects. The most picturesque spot for your grill may not be the most appropriate. Overhanging branches, for instance, may become kindling, confounding your efforts to confine your fire to the grill. Look for an open area with clearance for flare-ups. If you're using a portable grill, such as a tabletop model or a hibachi, raise it a foot or two above the ground on a fireproof surface, such as cinder blocks.

Make sure the site is outdoors. The unwary city dweller, in possession of a hibachi but short of open space, is often tempted by the windowsill and just as often treated to the piercing wail of the smoke detector and, possibly, a sensation of suffocating. It's easy to underestimate the volume of smoke generated by even the smallest grill, so it is advisable to grill only outdoors.

LIGHT THE FIRE WITH CAUTION

Avoid lighter fluids. Aside from adding an astringent flavor to foods at times, lighter fluids can cause flare-ups. Use solid starters instead. Altogether safe, they're widely available under various brand names. You'll find them virtually anywhere charcoal is sold.

Don't use paper as kindling. Stray bits may blow loose and scatter flames well beyond the bounds of your barbecue.

Have water within reach. A loaded water pistol (or spritzer bottle) is handy for subduing aggressive flames.

Have baking soda nearby. A box of baking soda will snuff out a fire.

With these basics at hand, please enjoy *Grilling from the Garden*.

CHAPTER 1

A Treasury of Vegetables

᠕

Grilling has meant meat for so long that to set about grilling vegetables is to blaze a trail through a wilderness of unmitigated delights. ᠕ For all the pleasures involved in the recent trend toward culinary sophistication, it has diminished our opportunities for fresh discovery. Happily, grilling vegetables offers a chance to enjoy flavors and sensations that are altogether new. When grilled, beets, potatoes, onions, and other vegetables taste like nothing else on earth. ᠕ What follows is a sampler featuring a variety of vegetables prepared simply, in ways that demonstrate how different—and how delicious—grilled vegetables can be. Some call for toppings and fillings such as chilies and russet potatoes, others for marinades, and several for nothing at all. I've found that most standard barbecue sauces overpower vegetables, which are more delicate than the hearty meat and poultry for which the sauces are intended. So here I've matched vegetables with basting preparations and marinades that best complement them. ᠕ One note before you begin: Many vegetables must be blanched before grilling, or they'll take forever to cook. When a recipe calls for blanching you can do it in the conventional way, by boiling or steaming briefly on top of the stove, or you can use a microwave. Blanching times will vary according to your method and the size of the vegetables. Unless the recipe specifies otherwise, whenever a vegetable is to be blanched, it should be cooked until a paring knife can *just* pierce through it.

ARTICHOKES

While they're commonly served boiled and bathed in marinade, artichoke hearts are never better, more buttery or full flavored, than when grilled.

SPECIAL EQUIPMENT: Wooden skewer soaked in water for 30 minutes before grilling

GRILL TEMPERATURE: High

6 medium artichokes
Marinade:
½ cup extra virgin olive oil
¼ cup fresh lemon juice
2 cloves garlic, crushed and minced
1 shallot, minced
Salt and freshly ground black pepper to taste
Mayonnaise (page 24, optional)

1. Boil or steam the artichokes until they're tender enough to strip easily, between 20 to 40 minutes depending on the size. Be careful not to let them get mushy, or the heart will come apart when you skewer it.

2. To make the marinade, combine the olive oil, lemon juice, garlic, shallot, and salt and pepper.

3. Drain the artichokes, strip the leaves down to the heart, remove and discard the fuzzy choke, and cut the heart in half.

4. Pour the marinade over the artichoke hearts and let them marinate for at least 3 hours.

5. Thread the hearts on a skewer and grill, turning once, until they've browned lightly, about 6 to 7 minutes.

6. Serve with Mayonnaise on the side as a dip.

23

MAYONNAISE

This mayonnaise recipe is also good with grilled asparagus, carrots, brussels sprouts, and potatoes. I wish I could give this sauce a new name, because it's nothing like what is commonly sold in supermarkets. The most I can do is tell you that it tastes different enough to justify the effort.

1 raw egg yolk
1 hard-boiled egg yolk
1¼ cups extra virgin olive oil
Salt to taste
1 clove garlic, crushed (optional)
¼ cup minced fresh chives or minced
  fresh cilantro (optional)

1. Using a blender or a food processor, combine the raw and cooked egg yolks until smooth.
2. With the blender running, add a third of the olive oil a drop at a time, making sure it binds with the yolks and forms a dense paste. As the paste thickens, add the remaining olive oil in a thin, steady stream, keeping the blender on throughout.
3. Season with salt, garlic, and chives or cilantro, if desired.

NOTE: If the ingredients fail to bind (as, I confess, mine sometimes do), you can fix it as follows: In a mixing bowl, combine 1 raw egg yolk and 2 tablespoons fresh lemon juice. Whisk in the mayonnaise mixture, stirring constantly until it binds. Correct seasoning to taste. Add one or more of the optional seasonings, if you'd like.

Makes about 1½ cups

ASPARAGUS

Asparagus abounds at the start of the grilling season, so here's how to make the most of this fortuitous timing. Be sure to handle asparagus with care; it tends to cook quickly.

GRILL TEMPERATURE: High

10–14 firm stalks asparagus
Marinade for artichokes (page 23)
Mayonnaise (page 24, optional)

1. Blanch the stalks until they're not quite cooked through. Steaming takes about 2 to 3 minutes, depending on how thick the stalks are. Be careful not to let them get limp at this stage; they'll become more tender on the grill.
2. Marinate them, refrigerated, for at least 3 hours.
3. Grill, turning the stalks often, until they're soft, but not mushy, about 2 minutes.
4. Serve with Mayonnaise for dipping, if desired.

AVOCADOS

Grilling accents the flavor and texture of this rich and hearty fruit.

GRILL TEMPERATURE: High

1 ripe but firm avocado, sliced into wedges about 1/3 inch thick
1 tablespoon fresh lemon juice
1 tablespoon fresh lime juice

1. Slice avocado into wedges 1/3 inch thick.
2. Combine the lemon juice and lime juice.
3. Brush each avocado wedge with the mixture. Grill immediately, turning once, until the slices are just lightly browned on the outside, and heated through, about 1 minute on each side.

Beets

Grilled beets have nothing in common with beets prepared any other way: crisp on the outside, tender and subtly sweet inside. If you think you don't like beets, suspend final judgment until you've tried these. Even if you like beets, you'll be startled to find they can be *this* good.

GRILL TEMPERATURE: High

6 beets, well scrubbed
Marinade:
4 tablespoons (¼ cup) unsalted butter
2 tablespoons honey
2 teaspoons grated fresh ginger

1. Boil the beets, whole, in a large saucepan for approximately 15 to 20 minutes, or cook them in the microwave until they're just tender enough to pierce with a paring knife. Drain and let them cool.
2. To make the marinade, combine the butter, honey, and ginger in a small saucepan. Heat gently, stirring until the butter has melted and the mixture is smooth.
3. When the beets are cool enough to handle, peel away the coarse outer layer, and slice them into rounds about ⅓ inch thick. Brush each round with the marinade.
4. Grill, turning once, until crisp on the outside yet still soft throughout, about 6 minutes on each side.

BROCCOLI

Grilling gives a beneficent boost to broccoli, amplifying its natural sweetness.

GRILL TEMPERATURE: High

1 bunch firm broccoli, trimmed
Marinade:
½ cup ginger vinegar or brown-rice
   vinegar
½ cup light soy sauce
¼ cup honey
1 clove garlic, crushed and minced
1 tablespoon lightly toasted sesame seeds

1. Blanch the broccoli in boiling water for 3 to 6 minutes or in the microwave until bright green, but not completely cooked.
2. To make the marinade, combine the vinegar, soy sauce, honey, garlic, and sesame seeds, and stir well.
3. Pour the marinade over the broccoli, refrigerate, and marinate for about 3 hours.
4. Grill on high heat, turning often, until just tender, about 5 to 6 minutes.

NOTE: To toast sesame seeds, heat oven to 350° F. Sprinkle sesame seeds on an ungreased baking sheet. Bake until lightly browned, about 3 to 5 minutes.

BRUSSELS SPROUTS

Brussels sprouts, which can be astringent, tend to mellow on the grill. Look for the tiny kind; they're sweet and tender and cook more quickly than the big, bulbous brussels sprouts.

SPECIAL EQUIPMENT: Wooden skewers soaked in water for 30 minutes before grilling

GRILL TEMPERATURE: High

2 cups brussels sprouts, trimmed
2 tablespoons unsalted butter, melted
1 tablespoon fresh orange juice
1 tablespoon sesame seeds

1. Blanch the brussels sprouts until they turn bright green and are soft enough to pierce with a skewer.
2. Meanwhile, combine the melted butter, orange juice, and sesame seeds.
3. Brush the brussels sprouts with the flavored butter and thread them on a skewer. Grill over high heat for about 6 minutes, rotating every minute or so to cook evenly.

CARROTS

Carrots remind me of the fad diets I followed in my teens. Basted with fine oil and fresh herbs and grilled over mesquite, these carrots aren't the least reminiscent of the flavorless sticks we ate by the pound, a perceived antidote to the chocolate we consumed in equal volume.

GRILL TEMPERATURE: High

8–10 small slender carrots, scraped
½ cup extra virgin olive oil
¼ cup balsamic vinegar
⅓ cup minced flat-leaf parsley
2 tablespoons fresh marjoram, minced
Salt and freshly ground black pepper to
   taste

1. Blanch the carrots until you can pierce them with a paring knife.
2. Meanwhile, combine the olive oil, vinegar, parsley, marjoram, and salt and pepper.
3. Brush the grill and the carrots with the oil mixture, and place the carrots directly on the grill. Cook over high heat, turning often, until soft, about 20 minutes.

CORN ON THE COB

Not the fastest nor the easiest way to cook corn on the cob, but surely among the tastiest.

GRILL TEMPERATURE: High

6 ears corn

One or more of the following (optional): salt to taste, ½ teaspoon cayenne pepper, 1 teaspoon paprika, 2 teaspoons finely minced fresh oregano, 2 teaspoons finely minced fresh basil, 2 teaspoons finely minced fresh chives

4 tablespoons (¼ cup) unsalted butter, softened

1. Husk the corn.
2. Combine the seasoning of your choice with the softened butter, if desired. Brush the butter onto the corn.
3. Wrap the ears of corn in a single layer of foil, and grill over high heat for 15 to 20 minutes, turning often.

CORN IN THE HUSK: Peel back the husk, taking care not to tear it off entirely. Combine the seasoning with the butter, if desired, and brush the butter onto the corn. Pull the husk back up over the corn and grill as in main recipe.

Eggplant

I've been eating grilled eggplant since childhood, when my grandfather used to thread it on skewers with lamb for shish kebab. Served with grilled peppers, onions, and tomatoes, it's as satisfying to me as it was when meat was in the mix. Use firm, glossy, slender eggplant, which tend to be sweeter and more tender than those that are squat and lusterless.

GRILL TEMPERATURE: Medium-high

1 eggplant

½ cup extra virgin olive oil

¼ cup dry white wine or balsamic vinegar

¼ cup finely crumbled Greek-style dried oregano

1 clove garlic, grated or finely minced

1. Trim and discard the stem and the base from the eggplant, and slice into rounds about ⅓ inch thick.

2. Combine the olive oil, vinegar, oregano, and garlic.

3. Brush the grill with regular olive oil to prevent sticking, and brush the eggplant with the seasoned oil mixture. Place the slices directly on the grill over medium-high heat and cook, turning them once halfway through, until very tender, about 7 to 12 minutes.

FENNEL

Fennel isn't as commonplace here as it is in Italy and France, where it sharpens up salads, sauces, and soups of all kinds. It's worth seeking out for its distinct licorice flavor, which mellows on the grill.

GRILL TEMPERATURE: High

1 medium bulb fennel
Marinade:
⅓ cup extra virgin olive oil
¼ cup dry white wine
Juice of 1 lemon
1 clove garlic, crushed and minced
¼ cup minced fresh parsley
Salt to taste
Grated imported Parmesan or Asiago
  cheese (optional)

1. Strip the leafy branches from the fennel, so only the bulb and stalks remain. Blanch the fennel in boiling water for 8 to 10 minutes or in the microwave until you can just pierce it with a paring knife. Drain and let it cool to room temperature.

2. To make the marinade, combine the olive oil, wine, lemon juice, garlic, parsley, and salt. Pour over the fennel.

3. Marinate, refrigerated, for at least 3 hours.

4. Place the fennel directly on the grill, over high heat, and grill, rotating often so it cooks evenly. It's ready when light brown on the outside and tender all the way through, about 8 to 12 minutes. Serve immediately, dusted with grated Parmesan or Asiago cheese, if desired.

31

GARLIC

Grilling tames this acrid herb, rendering it soft and mild. Grilled garlic is great spread on buttered toasted French bread.

GRILL TEMPERATURE: High

1 large clove garlic, unpeeled

1. Brush the grill with vegetable oil to prevent sticking. Place a whole, unpeeled garlic clove directly on the grill and grill over high heat until soft, about 6 to 8 minutes, turning it at least once.
2. Peel the garlic, mash it, and spread on toast as suggested above, or serve alongside a variety of vegetables. It's delicious with grilled potatoes.

LEEKS

For a less piquant version of grilled onions, try leeks, which grill up tender and sweet. You can sprinkle them with grated Parmesan cheese and serve them as a side dish with grilled tomatoes. (Save the green part to use as a seasoning for Vegetable Broth, see page 72.)

GRILL TEMPERATURE: High

4 leeks, white part only, sliced in half lengthwise

Brush the grill with vegetable oil to prevent sticking. Place the leeks directly on the grill and cook until they're soft, about 10 minutes, rotating them often.

MUSHROOMS

Basically bland, they absorb the complex flavors of whatever marinade you use.

GRILL TEMPERATURE: Medium-high

¼ cup fresh lemon juice

¼ cup pineapple juice

¼ cup minced scallions

2 teaspoons grated fresh ginger

2 tablespoons light soy sauce

2 tablespoons dry sherry

1 tablespoon raw sugar

1 pound fresh mushrooms of any kind (especially shiitake, oyster, wood ear, or, if you're lucky enough to have access to them, porcini)

1. In a small saucepan, combine the lemon juice, pineapple juice, scallions, ginger, soy sauce, sherry, and sugar. Heat gently until the sugar dissolves.

2. Transfer the mixture to a large bowl or a baking dish. Add the mushrooms and let them marinate, refrigerated, for at least 3 hours.

3. Brush the grill with vegetable oil to prevent sticking. Place the mushrooms stem side down on the grill over medium-high heat and cook until they're tender and golden brown around the edges, 8 to 15 minutes, depending on the size.

NOTE: This is a good recipe to try with flavored mesquite.

33

Onions

Onions grilled with fresh rosemary are uncommonly enticing.

GRILL TEMPERATURE: High

4 medium brown (Spanish) onions
⅓ cup extra virgin olive oil
Juice of ½ lemon
1 clove garlic, crushed and minced
1 tablespoon minced fresh rosemary
Salt and freshly ground black pepper to
    taste

1. Peel and quarter the onions.
2. Combine the olive oil, lemon juice, garlic, rosemary, and salt and pepper. Brush the onions with the seasoned oil mixture.
3. Brush the grill with vegetable oil to prevent sticking. Place the onions directly on the grill over high heat. Turn them while grilling until they're evenly browned, about 8 to 12 minutes.

NOTE: Vidalia onions deserve special treatment, see page 88.

Peppers

BELL PEPPERS

I've tried a number of marinades, but none improves the sweet and smoky flavor of unadorned bell peppers—red, yellow, or green—hot off the grill. I love them tossed into a salad with fresh herbs and soft, mild cheese (see page 55).

GRILL TEMPERATURE: High or medium

1 bell pepper

1. For each bell pepper, cut the pepper in half, and remove the core and seeds.
2. Brush the grill with vegetable oil so the pepper won't stick to it. Grill the pepper halves skin side up, about 1 minute, to soften. Turn them over and grill until the skin is charred, about 6 to 8 minutes more.

NOTE: You can serve the pepper as it is or do the following to remove the skin: Transfer the pepper to a paper bag while it's still hot, and let it steam until it's cool enough to handle, about 10 minutes. Peel away the skin and slice the pepper into strips.

CHILI PEPPERS

Served with a simple salad or soup, mild chilies filled with cheese make a fast, satisfying late supper.

GRILL TEMPERATURE: Medium-high

1 mild jalapeño, poblano, or Anaheim chili pepper, left whole

2 tablespoons (approximately) shredded cheese for each pepper (any prepared spiced cheese, such as Boursin with herbs, Monterey Jack with jalapeños, cheddar with herbs, Edam with caraway)

1. Brush the grill with vegetable oil to prevent sticking. Place the chilies directly on the grill over medium-high heat, and grill—turning the chilies often so they'll cook evenly—until they're just lightly charred, about 10 minutes.
2. Transfer them to a paper bag and let them steam until they're cool enough to handle, about 10 minutes.
3. Peel away the charred skin, taking care not to tear the walls.
4. Cut off the stem end of each and, using a teaspoon or a small butter knife, gently fill the cavity with cheese. Return the chilies to the grill until the cheese melts and begins to brown.

35

POTATOES

Considering how many ways we use them, it's hard to believe potatoes hold any surprises. But grilled spuds are astonishing: firm at first bite, tender and flavorful as you chew.

NEW POTATOES

Tiny new potatoes taste better and cook faster than the larger kind.

SPECIAL EQUIPMENT: Wooden skewers soaked in water for 30 minutes before grilling

GRILL TEMPERATURE: Medium-high

4 cups tiny new potatoes

6 tablespoons extra virgin olive oil

2 tablespoons fresh lemon juice

2 tablespoons minced fresh basil

1 tablespoon minced fresh oregano

1 tablespoon minced fresh rosemary

Salt and freshly ground black pepper to taste

1. Boil the potatoes until you can just pierce them with a skewer, about 4 to 6 minutes. (Do not let them get too soft, or they'll fall apart.)

2. Meanwhile, combine the olive oil, lemon juice, basil, oregano, rosemary, and salt and pepper.

3. Brush the grill with vegetable oil to prevent sticking. Thread the potatoes on a skewer, brush with the oil-and-herb mixture, and grill over medium-high heat, rotating the skewer often, until the potatoes' skins are light brown and crisp, and the insides are soft, about 8 to 12 minutes.

RUSSET POTATOES

Organic russets are much silkier and sweeter than conventionally grown potatoes.

GRILL TEMPERATURE: High

1 russet potato, unpeeled

1. Cut the potato lengthwise into slices about ¼ inch thick.

2. Brush the grill with vegetable oil to prevent sticking, and lay the slices on top. Cook over high heat, turning the slices every 4 to 5 minutes, until they're golden brown and tender, about 15 to 20 minutes.

❧

RUSSET POTATOES WITH CHEESE: Cut two potatoes almost in half lengthwise, but still attached along the bottom. Combine 2 tablespoons unsalted butter, softened and ¼ cup finely grated Gruyère or cheddar cheese. Using a butter knife, force a portion of the cheese mixture into the slit, and wrap each potato with foil. Place the potatoes on the grill, and cover with the grill lid or a tent of aluminum foil. Rotate the potatoes occasionally, so they'll cook evenly, about 60 to 90 minutes. They are done when they feel very soft.

SNOW PEAS

Better known as a staple in stir fries, snow peas grill up smoky and crisp.

SPECIAL EQUIPMENT: Fine-mesh grate

GRILL TEMPERATURE: Medium or low

¼ cup brown-rice vinegar
1 teaspoon dark sesame oil
1 teaspoon soy sauce
Pinch sugar
½ pound snow peas, stems and strings removed

1. Combine the vinegar, sesame oil, soy sauce, and sugar.
2. Pour the mixture over the snow peas, and let them marinate, refrigerated, for at least 3 hours.
3. Fit the grill with a fine-mesh grate. Brush the screen with vegetable oil to prevent sticking. Place the snow peas on top in a single layer. After 30 seconds, turn them over. (A wide spatula is perfect for this purpose.) After another 15 seconds remove them from the grill. Serve right away.

37
❧

Squash

Winter Squash (Acorn, Butternut, or Pumpkin)

I prefer grilled squash to squash prepared any other way. It's especially good when basted with butter and something sweet, such as marmalade or brown sugar.

GRILL TEMPERATURE: High

1 acorn squash, butternut squash, or
  small pumpkin

2 tablespoons unsalted butter

¼ cup raw sugar

3 tablespoons orange marmalade

1 tablespoon water

Pinch ground ginger

Pinch ground allspice

Pinch salt

Pinch finely ground black pepper

1. Cut the squash or pumpkin in half and scoop out the seeds. Cut it into quarters and steam or simmer it until you can just pierce the flesh with a sharp paring knife, about 8 minutes. Drain and let it cool.

2. Peel the squash or pumpkin and slice it into wedges about ⅓ inch thick.

3. Melt the butter in a small saucepan. Combine with sugar, marmalade, water, ginger, allspice, salt, and pepper. Heat gently, stirring until the sugar has dissolved and the mixture is smooth.

4. Brush the squash or pumpkin slices with the marmalade mixture.

5. Grill the squash or pumpkin slices, turning occasionally, until light brown on the surface and tender inside, about 8 to 10 minutes.

WINTER SQUASH WITH BROWN SUGAR: Prepare squash or pumpkin as directed in preceding squash recipe. Melt 6 tablespoons unsalted butter in small saucepan. Combine with 2 tablespoons of brown sugar and a pinch of ground cinnamon, ginger, and mace, and continue stirring over low heat, until the sugar melts. Brush the brown sugar mixture onto wedges of steamed squash or pumpkin, and grill as directed in preceding squash recipe.

SUMMER SQUASH (ZUCCHINI OR YELLOW)

By some miracle of chemistry, this insubstantial summer staple bounds off the grill, full of flavor and bite.

GRILL TEMPERATURE: High or medium

6 tablespoons extra virgin olive oil

2 tablespoons white wine vinegar

1 clove garlic, crushed and minced

1 tablespoon minced fresh oregano

Pinch salt

4 slender firm zucchini or yellow squash, cut into rounds ⅓ inch thick

Grated imported Parmesan or Asiago cheese (optional)

1. Combine the olive oil, vinegar, garlic, oregano, and salt.
2. Brush the grill with vegetable oil to prevent sticking, then brush the zucchini or yellow squash with the oil-and-herb mixture.
3. Place the zucchini or the yellow squash rounds on the grill in a single layer and cook over high or medium heat, turning occasionally, until very tender, about 8 to 12 minutes. Serve immediately, sprinkled with grated Parmesan or Asiago cheese, if you'd like.

Sweet Potatoes

Sweet potatoes are best when basted with cinnamon-spiced apple-maple syrup that gives them a golden brown crust when grilled. A toothsome treat that truly melts in your mouth.

GRILL TEMPERATURE: High

2 medium sweet potatoes
1 cup apple juice or filtered cider
3 tablespoons unsalted butter
2 teaspoons maple syrup
Pinch ground allspice
Pinch ground cinnamon
Pinch salt
Pinch finely ground black pepper

1. Peel the sweet potatoes and boil them whole until they're just tender enough to pierce with a paring knife, about 12 to 15 minutes. Drain them and let them rest until they're cool enough to handle.

2. Meanwhile, in a small saucepan, combine the apple juice or cider, butter, maple syrup, allspice, cinnamon, salt, and pepper. Heat gently, stirring until the butter melts and the mixture is smooth. Continue cooking, stirring often, until the mixture reduces by about a third.

3. Cut the potatoes lengthwise into slices about 1/3 inch thick. Brush the grill with vegetable oil to prevent sticking, and place the potatoes on top in a single layer. Brush the slices with the apple juice or cider mixture and grill—turning and basting often—until they're brown on the outside and tender throughout, about 10 minutes.

TOMATOES

Grilled tomatoes complement anything cooked outdoors.

GRILL TEMPERATURE: Medium-high

Ripe tomatoes

1. Brush the grill with olive oil to both season the tomatoes and prevent sticking.
2. Cut the tomatoes in half, and place them, skin side up, on the grill over medium-high heat. Cook until they've softened, about 5 minutes.
3. Turn the tomatoes over and grill them

41

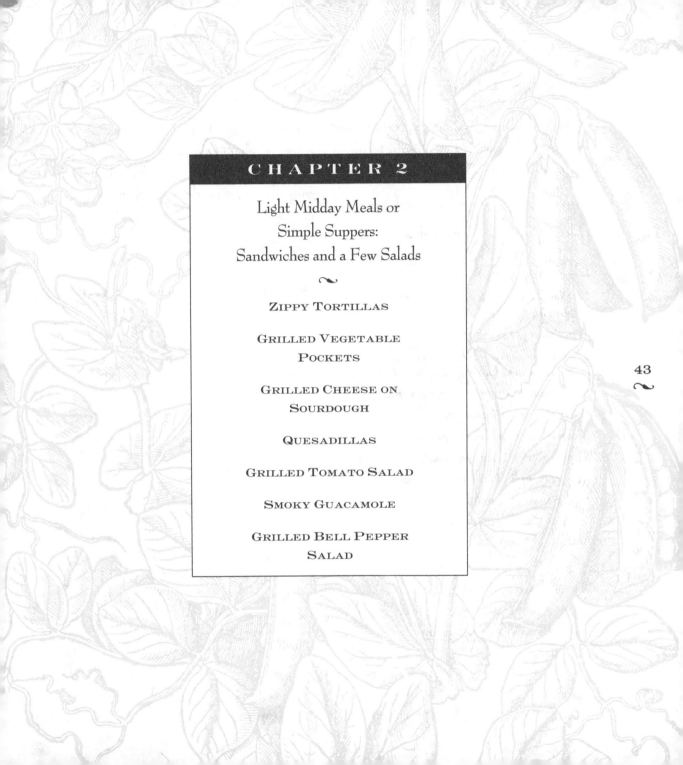

CHAPTER 2

Light Midday Meals or
Simple Suppers:
Sandwiches and a Few Salads

❧

ZIPPY TORTILLAS

GRILLED VEGETABLE
POCKETS

GRILLED CHEESE ON
SOURDOUGH

QUESADILLAS

GRILLED TOMATO SALAD

SMOKY GUACAMOLE

GRILLED BELL PEPPER
SALAD

ZIPPY TORTILLAS

"Zippy" in this case is doubly descriptive, referring to the taste of these terrific tortillas and to the time it takes to make them.

SPECIAL EQUIPMENT: Fine-mesh grate

GRILL TEMPERATURE: Medium

4 soft flour tortillas

1 cup Bean Puree (page 45) or prepared bean dip*

½ cup mild green salsa*

1 poblano or jalapeño chili pepper, grilled, peeled, and diced (page 35, steps 1–3)

¼ cup grated imported Parmesan cheese

¼ cup shredded cheddar cheese

¼ cup shredded Monterey Jack cheese

Minced fresh cilantro (optional)

1 avocado, grilled and diced (optional)

Sour cream (optional)

Tomato salsa* (optional)

1. Spread each tortilla with ¼ cup Bean Puree or bean dip and ⅛ cup green salsa. Sprinkle each evenly with the diced chilies, and the Parmesan, cheddar, and Monterey Jack cheese.

2. Place the tortillas on the grill, cover loosely with foil tents, and cook until the bottoms are seared and the cheese is slightly melted, about 1 minute.
3. Serve immediately, garnished, if desired, with cilantro, avocado, sour cream, or tomato salsa.

Serves 2 to 4

*SEE APPENDIX FOR MAIL-ORDER SOURCES.

Bean Puree

2 tablespoons corn oil (unrefined, if available)
1 clove garlic, crushed and minced
½ cup finely chopped red onion
1 tablespoon tomato paste
2 tablespoons water
2 teaspoons ground cumin powder
1 teaspoon powdered oregano
1 teaspoon chili powder (or more, to taste)
½ teaspoon cayenne pepper
1 cup canned or freshly cooked pinto or kidney beans, drained and mashed

1. Heat the corn oil in a skillet, and sauté the garlic and onion until soft, about 7 minutes.
2. Add the tomato paste, water, cumin, oregano, chili powder, and cayenne pepper, and stir until well blended. Add the beans and stir again until smooth.
3. Remove from the heat and let cool to room temperature. If desired, cover and refrigerate until ready to use, up to 4 days.

Makes about 1 cup

∾

Fresh Raspberry Sauce

A refreshing, versatile topping—stir it into plain or lemon yogurt, or spoon it over vanilla ice cream or lime sorbet.

2 cups fresh raspberries
½ teaspoon grated lemon zest
¼ cup superfine sugar

1. Press the raspberries through a sieve into a mixing bowl.
2. Stir in the lemon zest and sugar. Mix well.
3. Cover and refrigerate until ready to use, up to 3 days.

Makes about 2 cups

GRILLED VEGETABLE POCKETS

A perfect summer supper: pita pockets stuffed with crisp, smoky vegetables, and for dessert ambrosial fresh berry soup.

SPECIAL EQUIPMENT: Fine-mesh grate

GRILL TEMPERATURE: High

2 stalks broccoli, cut into bite-size pieces

2 large carrots, scraped, sliced into wafer-thin rounds

1 cup sliced red onion, loosely packed

⅓ cup extra virgin olive oil

2 tablespoons dry white wine

1 tablespoon minced fresh oregano, or 1 teaspoon crumbled dried oregano

1 teaspoon freshly ground black pepper

½ teaspoon salt

1 slender Japanese eggplant, sliced into ½-inch rounds

8 cherry tomatoes

1 cup snow peas, loosely packed, stems and strings removed

1 small red bell pepper, cored, seeded, and cut into wide strips

1 clove garlic, peeled

2 8-inch pita pockets

Sandwich Spread (page 47)

Alfalfa sprouts

1. In boiling water, blanch the broccoli until it turns bright green, about 3 minutes, or blanch it in the microwave.

2. In boiling water, blanch the carrots until softened, about 4 minutes, or blanch them in the microwave.

3. In boiling water, blanch the onion until softened, about 3 minutes, or blanch it in the microwave.

4. In a large glass or earthenware mixing bowl, combine the olive oil, wine, oregano, pepper, and salt. Add the blanched vegetables as well as the eggplant, cherry tomatoes, snow peas, bell pepper, and garlic. Toss well to thoroughly coat the vegetables.

5. Cover and refrigerate for at least 3 hours.

6. Spread the vegetables on the fine-mesh grate, grouping them by type, and grill until they're cooked through, about 8 to 12 minutes. Remove them from the grill as soon

as they're done. Cooking time for each type of vegetable will vary, but you can tell when they are done by piercing a knife through them. The eggplant, onions, and broccoli should be soft, the carrots and peas should be crisp, and the tomatoes and pepper should be charred. Strip away the charred skin from the pepper before serving, and mash the garlic clove well.

7. Split each pita round into two pockets. Spread with Sandwich Spread, and line with alfalfa sprouts. Fill with the grilled vegetables.

8. Return the pockets to the grill briefly to heat through, and serve at once.

Serves 2

SANDWICH SPREAD

1 cup plain yogurt (nonfat, if desired)
1 tablespoon toasted or regular tahini*
1 tablespoon fresh lemon juice
1 teaspoon ground cumin
1 teaspoon paprika
Pinch salt

1. Line a colander with absorbent paper towels or a coffee filter. Pour in the yogurt and let it drain, refrigerate, until you have something the consistency of cream cheese, about 8 hours.

2. In a mixing bowl, combine the tahini and lemon juice and stir until smooth. Stir in the cumin, paprika, and salt. Add the drained yogurt, and mix well to blend.

3. Store in the refrigerator up to 4 days until ready to use.

Makes about ⅓ cup or enough for 2 sandwiches

*SEE APPENDIX FOR MAIL-ORDER SOURCES.

47

Cold and Creamy Berry Soup

1 pint blueberries or very ripe strawberries, washed and hulled

1⅔ cups water

½ cup honey or maple syrup

1 cup plain yogurt, buttermilk, or sour cream

Ground cinnamon (optional)

1. In a medium saucepan, combine the berries, water, and honey or maple syrup. Heat to a gentle simmer, and let the mixture cook, stirring occasionally, until the fruit breaks down into a soup, about 15 to 20 minutes.

2. Puree the mixture in a food processor or blender. Add the yogurt, buttermilk, or sour cream, and blend again just to combine.

3. Season with cinnamon, if desired. Cover and refrigerate the soup until well chilled, at least 3 hours.

Serves 4

48

GRILLED CHEESE ON SOURDOUGH

Good and gooey grilled cheese can make a mess, one which peels off easily if you've brushed the grate lightly with oil before grilling and clean up promptly.

SPECIAL EQUIPMENT: Fine-mesh grate

GRILL TEMPERATURE: Medium or low

Mustard Dressing (right)
2 thin slices sourdough bread
4 thin slices tomato (optional)
1 bell pepper, grilled (pages 34-35, optional), or jalapeño pepper, grilled (page 35, optional)
⅓ cup shredded sharp cheddar cheese or Monterey Jack, Colby, or cheddar cheese with jalapeños

1. Spread the Mustard Dressing on one slice of bread. Top with tomato and pepper, if desired.
2. Brush the fine-mesh grate lightly with vegetable oil, and lay the cheese on top. Next to the cheese, place the slice of bread, tomato side up. Grill until the cheese starts to melt and the bread starts to brown lightly. Using the spatula, scrape off the cheese and spread it on the bread.
3. Top the sandwich with the other slice of bread. Grill the sandwich to toast the other side, about 30 seconds.

Serves 1

MUSTARD DRESSING

½ cup dried apricots or dried peaches
Fresh orange juice to cover (about ⅔ cup)
2 tablespoons grainy prepared mustard
1 teaspoon honey

1. In a small saucepan, heat the dried fruit and orange juice. Simmer gently until the fruit is soft and plump, about 10 minutes.
2. Drain well. Puree the fruit along with the juice in a food processor or blender. Transfer it to a small mixing bowl.
3. Add the mustard and honey, and stir until well combined.

Makes about ¼ cup

∾

CARROT AND RAISIN SLAW

A refreshing take on a summer-time standard.

1½ cups shredded carrots
1½ cups shredded white cabbage
1 cup golden raisins
1 Granny Smith apple, peeled, cored, and grated
1 tablespoon fresh lemon juice
2 teaspoons honey
1 tablespoon finely shredded unsweetened coconut
1 cup plain yogurt, or ½ cup plain yogurt and ½ cup sour cream
¼ cup chopped walnuts (optional)

1. Combine the carrots, cabbage, raisins, and apple.
2. In a separate bowl, whisk together the lemon juice, honey, coconut, and yogurt or yogurt–sour cream mixture.
3. Combine the cabbage mixture and the dressing, and toss thoroughly. Add the walnuts, if desired, and stir until they're well distributed.
4. Refrigerate the slaw until it's thoroughly chilled, about 3 hours. It will keep for up to 3 days.

Serves 4 to 6

QUESADILLAS

Try it once and you'll find that this tasty, simple, tortilla-based supper is a fine incentive for keeping your condiment shelf well stocked, and a ripe avocado ever on hand.

SPECIAL EQUIPMENT: Fine-mesh grate

GRILL TEMPERATURE: Low

1 tablespoon Cilantro Pesto (page 52)

2 flour tortillas (6 inch diameter)

1–2 teaspoons Mango Catsup (page 52), or 1 teaspoon prepared green salsa* and several thin slices peeled ripe mango or peach

¼ cup shredded Monterey Jack cheese

1. Spread a thin layer of Cilantro Pesto on one tortilla. Spread the Mango Catsup or green salsa on top. If you're using fresh mango or peach slices, distribute them evenly over the salsa.
2. Sprinkle the Monterey Jack cheese on the other tortilla.
3. Place each tortilla on the grill and cover loosely with foil. Grill just until the cheese starts to melt, about 1½ to 2 minutes. Check often.
4. Flip the pesto-spread tortilla on top of the other to sandwich the fillings. Grill, uncovered, briefly (about 15 to 20 seconds) on one side, turn over, and grill briefly on the other.
5. Cut into wedges and serve immediately.

Serves 1

*SEE APPENDIX FOR MAIL-ORDER SOURCES.

51

Cilantro Pesto

Pungent cilantro replaces the conventional basil for a delicious Southwestern twist on a favorite summertime sauce.

1 clove garlic, mashed
2 tablespoons corn oil (unrefined, if available)
½ cup minced fresh cilantro
¼ cup grated imported Parmesan cheese

1. Using a mortar and pestle, a food processor, or a blender fixed with a small container, grind together the garlic and corn oil.
2. Add the cilantro and cheese, and grind to a dense paste. It will keep refrigerated for up to 3 days.

Makes about ⅓ cup or enough for 4 quesadillas

❧

Mango Catsup

Ready-made condiments are easy to come by, but this sensational sweet-and-sour sauce is well worth making yourself.

4 medium ripe mangoes, peeled and chopped
¼ cup dry white wine
¼ cup light brown sugar
2 tablespoons apple cider vinegar
2 teaspoons ground ginger
Pinch ground cinnamon
Pinch ground cloves
Pinch ground allspice

1. Place all of the ingredients in a food processor or blender, and puree.
2. Transfer to a saucepan and bring the mixture to a simmer, stirring occasionally. Let the catsup simmer until it thickens and reduces by half, about an hour.
3. Remove it from the heat and let it cool completely. Refrigerate for at least 8 hours before serving, allowing time for the flavors to blend. The catsup will keep, refrigerated, for up to 3 weeks.

Makes about 1¼ cups

❧

Chilled Avocado Soup

Fresh sharp herbs and tangy buttermilk enliven this creamy chilled soup.

1 large ripe avocado, peeled, pitted, and sliced

2 tablespoons finely minced scallion, white part only

3 cups buttermilk, or 1 ½ cups each plain yogurt and buttermilk, whisked together until smooth

1 tablespoon minced fresh chives or dill

Salt and freshly ground black pepper to taste

1. In a food processor or blender, combine the avocado, scallion, buttermilk or yogurt and buttermilk, and herbs. Process until smooth.

2. Season with salt and pepper, cover, and refrigerate until well chilled, about 3 hours.

Serves 4 to 6

SUMMER SALAD SAMPLER

❧

An appealing array of grilled vegetables.
Serve these salads together for a light lunch, or separately as side dishes.

GRILLED TOMATO SALAD

A dish to savor when tomatoes reach their peak.

*4 tomatoes, grilled, peeled, and chopped
(page 41)*

*1 clove garlic, grilled, peeled, and mashed
(page 32)*

1 leek, grilled and chopped (page 32)

1/3 cup crumbled feta cheese

1/4 cup chopped black olives

1 tablespoon capers

1/4 cup minced fresh parsley

Salt and freshly ground black pepper to taste

Extra virgin olive oil to taste

Combine the tomatoes, garlic, leek, feta cheese, olives, capers, and parsley. Season with salt and pepper and toss with the olive oil. Serve immediately.

Serves 2 to 4

SMOKY GUACAMOLE

Spirited salsa chimes in with mellow grilled avocado in this whimsical variation on a familiar theme.

1 avocado, grilled (page 25)

1 clove garlic, grilled and peeled (page 32)

*1 teaspoon Pungent Pepper Sauce (page 60)
or store-bought salsa*

*1 tablespoon minced fresh cilantro
(optional)*

Dash cayenne pepper

Salt to taste

Fresh lemon juice to taste

Mash together all of the ingredients. Serve immediately, or wrap and store in the refrigerator for up to 3 days.

Makes about 1 cup

GRILLED BELL PEPPER SALAD

The quality of this salad depends entirely on the quality of its ingredients. Choose firm, unblemished peppers, garden-fresh herbs, and verdant oil.

2 yellow or orange bell peppers, grilled and sliced into strips (pages 34-35)

2 red bell peppers, grilled and sliced into strips (pages 34-35)

2 tablespoons minced fresh chives

2 tablespoons minced fresh mint

2 to 3 tablespoons extra virgin olive oil

Toss the bell peppers with the chives and mint. Drizzle with the olive oil and toss again. Serve immediately.

Serves 2 to 4

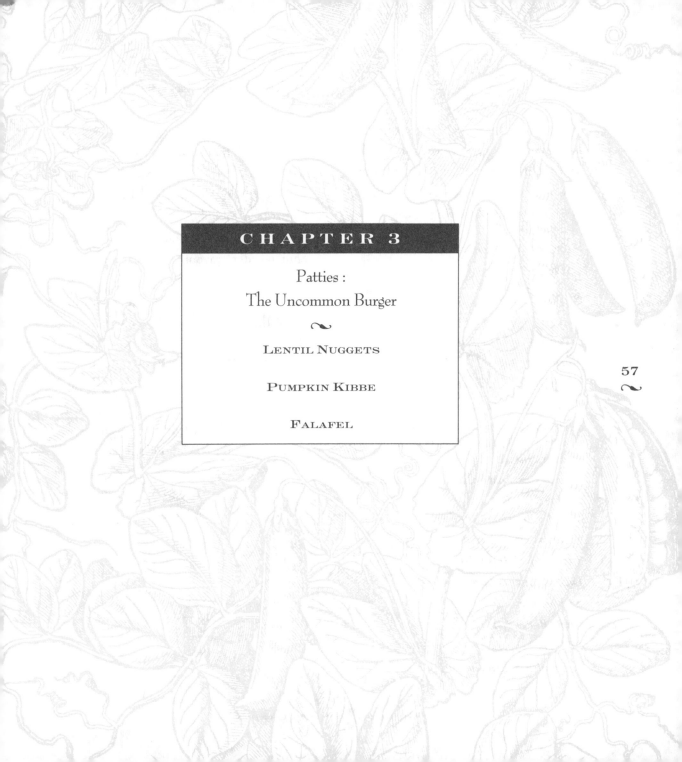

CHAPTER 3

Patties :
The Uncommon Burger

∾

LENTIL NUGGETS

PUMPKIN KIBBE

FALAFEL

Lentil Nuggets

These boldly spiced patties are really just an excuse for sampling condiments of all kinds. However, the delicious lentil mixture asserts its potent good flavor through sweet and pungent toppings alike.

Special Equipment: Wire-mesh grill screen (optional)

Grill Temperature: Medium

½ cup brown lentils, rinsed

1 dried bay leaf

¼ cup finely diced white onion

1 clove garlic, crushed and minced

½ cup whole wheat couscous or fine bulgur wheat, cooked according to package directions

1 small russet potato, baked, peeled, and mashed

2 teaspoons ground cumin

1 teaspoon crumbled dried thyme

1 teaspoon chili powder

Dash cayenne pepper

Salt to taste

Apple Butter (page 59)

Pungent Pepper Sauce (page 60)

Red Onion Relish (page 61)

1. Place the lentils, bay leaf, and onion in a saucepan with enough water to cover. Bring to a gentle boil, cover with a lid, and simmer until the lentils are tender and the water has been absorbed, about 30 minutes.
2. Discard the bay leaf and transfer the lentils to a mixing bowl. Add the garlic, couscous or bulgur, potato, cumin, thyme, chili powder, cayenne pepper, and salt. Mix well.
3. Shape the mixture into plump ovals about the size of your palm and place inside a wire-mesh grill screen or lay directly on the grill. Cook 15 to 20 minutes, turning once, until they've browned evenly on both sides.
4. Serve with Apple Butter, Pungent Pepper Sauce, and Red Onion Relish.

Serves 6

APPLE BUTTER

A perfect—modifying—complement to the spicy nuggets.

1 cup filtered apple juice

1 cup dried apples (organic, if you can find them)

8 pounds firm cooking apples (such as Rome, Winesap, or Cortland), peeled, cored, and chopped

1 cup water

1 tablespoon grated lemon zest

1 tablespoon fresh lemon juice

2 tablespoons light brown sugar

2 teaspoons ground cinnamon

1 teaspoon ground ginger

½ teaspoon ground cloves

½ teaspoon ground allspice

1. Bring the apple juice to a boil. Place the dried apples in a glass or ceramic bowl and pour the hot apple juice over them. Let them sit until plump, about an hour.

2. Place the cooking apples and the plumped dried apples with the juice in a large kettle or Dutch oven. Add approximately 1 cup of water or enough to come about 1 inch up the side of the pan.

3. Bring the water to a gentle boil, cover, and reduce the heat. Simmer until the apples are soft, about 45 minutes, stirring occasionally. Check the water level often, adding more as needed, a tablespoon at a time, to prevent burning.

4. Transfer the apples to a food processor or blender, and puree, taking care not to liquefy. Pour the mixture into a saucepan and stir in the lemon zest, lemon juice, brown sugar, cinnamon, ginger, cloves, and allspice.

5. Cook over low heat, stirring often, until the mixture thickens and reduces by about a third, about 10 to 15 minutes. Remove from the heat and let cool completely. Refrigerate for at least 8 hours before serving, allowing time for the flavors to meld. Store in the refrigerator for up to 3 weeks.

Makes about 4 cups

PUNGENT PEPPER SAUCE

A novel salsa when made with yellow cherry tomatoes, which taste slightly sharper than the red variety.

1 pound cherry tomatoes or yellow cherry tomatoes

1 shallot, finely minced

1 clove garlic, crushed and minced

2 tablespoons fresh minced cilantro

2 serrano chili peppers, seeded, roasted, skinned, and minced (page 35)

1 tablespoon fresh lime juice

Salt to taste

Toss all of the ingredients into the blender or food processor and process in spurts to chop fine. Be careful not to liquefy. It will keep, refrigerated, for up to 3 days.

Makes about 1 cup

RED ONION RELISH

This sweet-and-sour condiment is sensational. If you've never tried dried cherries, here's your chance to discover that, unlike raisins, which taste nothing like grapes, dried cherries taste intensely of the fruit.

3 large red onions, sliced into
    thin rings
1/4 cup extra virgin olive oil
1 tablespoon raw sugar
1/3 cup dried cherries* or raisins
1/2 cup raspberry vinegar

1. Soak the onion slices in cold water for an hour. Drain, and blot dry.
2. In a small saucepan, combine the olive oil and sugar. Heat gently, stirring until the sugar dissolves. Add the onion and cook over low heat until the onion goes limp, about 15 minutes.
3. Stir in the cherries or raisins and vinegar, and simmer over medium heat until most of the liquid evaporates and the onion virtually melts. Let cool to room temperature. It will keep, refrigerated, for up to 3 days.

Makes about 2 cups

* SEE APPENDIX FOR MAIL-ORDER SOURCES.

Pumpkin Kibbe

This admittedly odd-seeming meal may appear to be a daring departure from conventional barbecue fare, but it's actually a justly time-honored recipe from the Middle East, where kibbe, a loosely defined dish, is made with lamb, beef, wheat, or pumpkin. It can be deep-fried, pan-fried, baked, left raw—or grilled, of course.

SPECIAL EQUIPMENT: Wire-mesh grill screen (optional)

GRILL TEMPERATURE: Medium

½ cup pumpkin puree

1 egg, beaten

⅓ cup diced yellow onion

½ cup fine bulgur wheat or whole wheat couscous, cooked according to package directions

1 medium russet potato, baked, peeled, and mashed

2 teaspoons ground cumin

1 teaspoon ground cinnamon

½ teaspoon ground allspice

Pinch salt

Freshly ground black pepper to taste

¼ cup walnuts, finely chopped

¼ cup currants

2 8-inch pita pockets

Cranberry Catsup (page 63)

1. In a medium mixing bowl, stir the pumpkin and egg together until well combined.

2. Add the onion, bulgur or couscous, potato, cumin, cinnamon, allspice, salt, and pepper. Mix thoroughly, using your hands.

3. Shape into small, plump patties, about 2 inches in diameter.

4. Combine the walnuts and currants. Press 1 tablespoon of this mixture into the center of each kibbe.

5. Place the kibbe on a wire-mesh grill screen, or lay them directly on the grill. Cover and cook over medium heat, turning once, until the kibbe have browned evenly on both sides, approximately 4 to 5 minutes on each side.

6. Serve in pita pockets, topped with Cranberry Catsup.

Serves 2

CRANBERRY CATSUP

The word *catsup* refers to any sweet sauce served in a highly concentrated form. Hence, cranberry most definitely qualifies here.

1 cup fresh or frozen cranberries
1 cup light honey
1 cup water
2 tablespoons apple cider vinegar
½ cup dried cherries
3 thin slices red onion
1 stick cinnamon
1 whole clove
2 teaspoons grated lemon zest

1. Combine all of the ingredients in a saucepan and bring to a boil. Simmer, stirring often, until the cranberries cook down, the cherries plump, and the onion softens, about 30 minutes. Continue simmering until the mixture thickens and reduces by half, about another 15 minutes.

2. Remove and discard the cinnamon stick and the clove. Transfer the mixture to a food processor or blender. Process until smooth.

3. Let cool completely, then cover and refrigerate for at least 8 hours before serving, allowing time for the flavors to meld. This catsup can be stored in the refrigerator for up to 3 weeks.

Makes about ¾ cup

Mixed Greens with Citrus Dressing

This delicious dressing is virtually fat-free.

*2 tablespoons fresh orange or
    lemon juice*

Splash balsamic vinegar

1 teaspoon honey

1 tablespoon minced fresh chives

*1 small clove garlic, crushed and
    minced*

1 teaspoon Dijon mustard

½ cup plain yogurt

*Salt and freshly ground black
    pepper to taste*

*6 cups (approximately) mixed
    greens of your choice, such as
    Boston lettuce, arugula,
    escarole, spinach, endive*

1. In a small bowl, whisk together the orange or lemon juice, vinegar, honey, chives, garlic, and mustard. Whisk in the yogurt, and season with salt and pepper.
2. Pour the dressing over the greens, toss, and serve. The dressing will keep in the refrigerator for up to 4 days.

Serves 4 to 6

Falafel

Grilled falafel tastes much better, and is healthier than the conventional deep-fried version of the dish. I love it spread with tahini, topped with the zesty Tomato Relish, and served with the tart Spinach and Yogurt Salad.

SPECIAL EQUIPMENT: Wire-mesh grill screen (optional)

GRILL TEMPERATURE: Medium

1 medium russet potato, baked, peeled, and mashed

3 cups cooked chick-peas, drained and mashed

2 tablespoons toasted or regular tahini*

1 tablespoon plain yogurt

½ cup soft whole wheat bread crumbs

⅔ cup finely chopped red onion

2 cloves garlic, crushed and minced

1 tablespoon ground cumin

2 teaspoons sweet paprika

Dash cayenne pepper

Pinch salt

¼ cup minced fresh cilantro

6 mini pita pockets or whole wheat burger buns

Tahini Spread (page 66)

Tomato Relish (page 66)

1. In a large mixing bowl, combine the potato, chick-peas, tahini, yogurt, bread crumbs, onion, garlic, cumin, paprika, cayenne pepper, salt, and cilantro. Mix well, using your hands, until thoroughly blended.

2. Shape the mixture into 6 patties and place inside a wire-mesh grill screen or directly on the grill. Cook for about 15 minutes, turning once halfway through, until they've browned evenly. Do not overcook.

3. Serve in pita pockets or burger buns, with Tahini Spread and Tomato Relish on top.

Serves 6

*SEE APPENDIX FOR MAIL-ORDER SOURCES.

TAHINI SPREAD

¼ cup toasted or regular tahini*
1 tablespoon hot water
2 tablespoons fresh lemon juice
¼ cup plain yogurt
½ clove garlic, crushed and minced
Salt to taste

1. Make a smooth paste by combining the tahini, hot water, and lemon juice.
2. Whisk in the yogurt, garlic, and salt. It will keep refrigerated for up to 4 days.

Makes about ½ cup

*SEE APPENDIX FOR MAIL-ORDER SOURCES.

TOMATO RELISH

1 tablespoon ground cumin
2 large ripe tomatoes, peeled, seeded, drained, and chopped
1 small white onion, chopped
3 tablespoons minced fresh cilantro
Pinch cayenne pepper
Salt to taste

1. Heat the oven to 250° F. Place the cumin on a sheet of foil and toast until it turns a deep brown, about 3 minutes. Watch carefully to make sure it doesn't blacken and burn.
2. Toss the tomatoes with the onion, cilantro, cayenne pepper, and the toasted cumin. Season with salt.

Makes about 2 cups

66

Spinach and Yogurt Salad

½ pound fresh spinach
1 cup plain yogurt
2 tablespoons fresh lemon juice
1 teaspoon grated onion
1 tablespoon minced fresh mint
Salt and freshly ground black
*   pepper to taste*

1. Wash the spinach thoroughly, and place it in a skillet while still wet. Heat gently, turning once or twice, until the leaves are soft and cooked through, about 1 to 2 minutes. Remove from the heat.
2. Squeeze the spinach dry, and chop well.
3. In a mixing bowl, whisk the yogurt until smooth and light. Stir in the lemon juice, onion, mint, and spinach. Season with salt and pepper.
4. Refrigerate until chilled through, at least 3 hours.

Serves 4

CHAPTER 4

En Brochette:

Supper on a Skewer

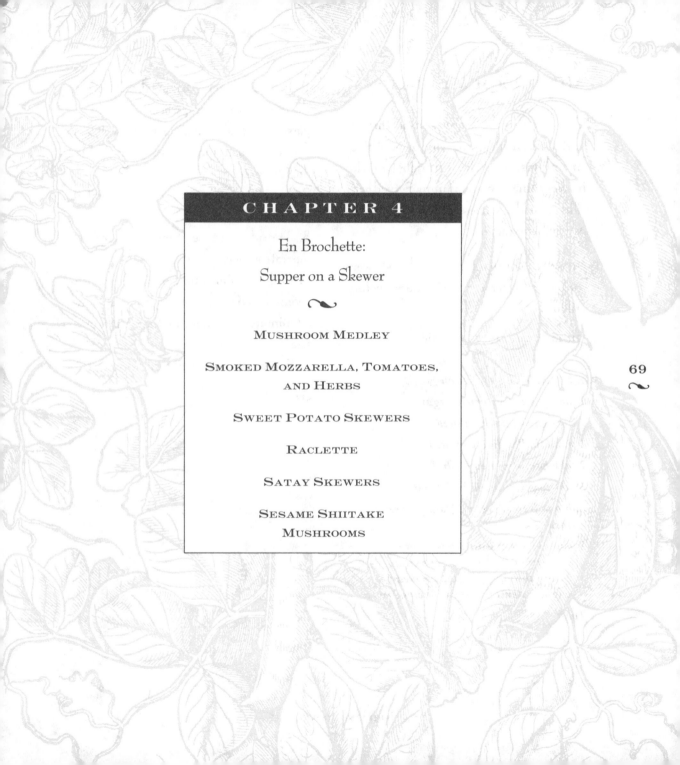

MUSHROOM MEDLEY

SMOKED MOZZARELLA, TOMATOES,
AND HERBS

SWEET POTATO SKEWERS

RACLETTE

SATAY SKEWERS

SESAME SHIITAKE
MUSHROOMS

Mushroom Medley

Grilling tames the sharp herbs in this flavorful marinade, rendering a soothing, smooth-tasting dish, just right for the brisk evenings of early autumn. Served with silky Cheddar Cheese Soup, it's an altogether satisfying meal.

SPECIAL EQUIPMENT: Wooden skewers soaked in water for 30 minutes before grilling

GRILL TEMPERATURE: High

½ cup extra virgin olive oil

2 tablespoons balsamic vinegar

1 clove garlic, finely minced

1 small shallot, finely minced

2 tablespoons minced fresh chives

2 tablespoons minced fresh parsley

Salt and freshly ground black pepper to taste

2 pounds total at least 3 types fresh mushrooms (such as white button, oyster, shiitake, porcini, wood ear) washed, stems trimmed if necessary

Toast

1. In a large bowl or baking dish, combine the olive oil, vinegar, garlic, shallot, chives, parsley, and salt and pepper. Stir well, and add the mushrooms, tossing until thoroughly coated.

2. Marinate the mushrooms, refrigerated, for at least 3 hours.

3. Thread each type of mushroom onto a separate skewer.

4. Grill, turning often, until the mushrooms are cooked through, between 8 and 12 minutes, depending on the mushrooms, size.

5. Serve spooned over toast.

Serves 4

CHEDDAR CHEESE SOUP

You'll enjoy this hearty soup long after you've stashed away the grill for the season. Remember, the soup will be as good as the cheddar you put into it, so choose a cheese accordingly.

2 tablespoons unsalted butter

2 tablespoons unbleached white flour

1 cup hot milk

2 cups hot Vegetable Broth (page 72)

1 cup shredded cheddar cheese, or ½ cup shredded cheddar cheese and ½ cup shredded cheddar cheese with jalapeños

1. In a heavy saucepan, melt the butter. Stir in the flour and cook briefly over low heat until a paste forms and it just starts to darken.
2. Pour in the milk and stir constantly until the mixture thickens and reduces by approximately half, about 10 minutes.
3. Add the hot broth and cook, stirring, until thickened, about 7 minutes more. Stir in the cheese, and cook until everything's smooth and well combined, about 5 minutes. Serve immediately.

Serves 4 to 6

VEGETABLE BROTH

*4 large carrots, scraped and
 sliced*

*1 large yellow onion, peeled and
 thinly sliced*

*1 large bulb fennel, including
 leaves, coarsely chopped, or 4
 large stalks celery, including
 leaves, chopped*

*4 cloves garlic, crushed and
 minced*

*2 medium red potatoes,
 quartered*

1 fresh or dried bay leaf

*Generous pinch minced fresh
 oregano, basil, and thyme, or
 2 teaspoons dried crumbled
 oregano, basil, and thyme*

*Salt and freshly ground black
 pepper to taste*

8 cups water

1. In a large kettle or Dutch oven, combine all of the ingredients. Bring to a boil, cover, and lower the heat. Simmer, covered, for 1½ hours.

2. Line a colander with cheese-cloth, and strain the broth through it. Either discard the vegetables, or puree half of them with the broth for a thicker stock.

3. If you're not going to use the broth right away, store it in the refrigerator for up to 3 days, or freeze it for up to 3 months.

Makes about 8 cups

Smoked Mozzarella, Tomatoes, and Herbs

Simply sublime.

Special Equipment: Fine-mesh grate, wooden skewers soaked in water for 30 minutes before grilling

Grill Temperature: High

¼ cup extra virgin olive oil
1 clove garlic, finely minced
1 small shallot, finely minced
2 tablespoons minced fresh basil
16 cherry tomatoes
2 cups cubed smoked mozzarella

1. Combine the olive oil, garlic, shallot, and basil.
2. Alternating tomatoes and cheese, thread them onto the skewers.
3. Brush the skewers and the grill with the oil-and-herb mixture.
4. Grill on a fine-mesh grate, turning often, until the tomatoes char lightly and the cheese gets gooey, about 6 to 8 minutes.

Serves 4 to 6

73

Chilled Chick-Pea Salad

This sweet and crunchy combo is one of my favorite summertime side dishes.

2 tablespoons extra virgin olive oil

1 clove garlic, crushed and minced

½ cup chopped red onion

2 cups cooked chick-peas

2 tablespoons minced fresh parsley

1 tablespoon red wine vinegar

¼ cup raisins or dried cranberries

¼ cup lightly toasted pine nuts or lightly toasted slivered almonds

2 tablespoons fresh orange juice

Salt and freshly ground black pepper to taste

1. In a skillet, heat the olive oil and sauté the garlic and onion until the onion softens and turns translucent, about 8 minutes.

2. Stir in the chick-peas and parsley, and continue to cook over low heat until the chick-peas are evenly coated with herbs. Remove the mixture from the heat and transfer to a mixing bowl.

3. Add the vinegar, raisins or cranberries, pine nuts or almonds, and orange juice. Toss well. Season with salt and pepper, and serve at room temperature, or chill and serve cold.

Serves 4 to 6

NOTE: Spread pine nuts or almonds on baking sheet. Bake until lightly browned, 4 to 6 minutes.

Sweet Potato Skewers

It's too bad that prunes are primarily associated with their medicinal properties, because that seems to keep many cooks from using them. If you're one of those cooks, try this delicious dish, in which prunes lend their deep, winy taste to maple-glazed sweet potatoes.

SPECIAL EQUIPMENT: Wooden skewers soaked in water for 30 minutes before grilling

GRILL TEMPERATURE: High

1 cup pitted prunes
2 large sweet potatoes
Maple Glaze (page 76)
Cool Cardamom Dressing (page 76), 1
    recipe

1. Place the prunes in a bowl and pour boiling water over them. Cover and let rest until the prunes plump up, about 30 minutes. Drain well.
2. Meanwhile, boil the sweet potatoes until they're just cooked through, about 15 minutes. Drain, and let them cool to room temperature, then peel and cut them into chunks.
3. Brush the prunes and potatoes with Maple Glaze.
4. Alternating prunes and potatoes, thread them onto the skewers.
5. Grill, turning the skewers often, until a crisp coating forms, about 12 minutes.
6. Drizzle Cool Cardamom Dressing lightly over the sweet potatoes and prunes. Serve immediately.

Serves 4 to 6

MAPLE GLAZE

4 tablespoons (¼ cup) unsalted
   butter
¼ cup maple syrup
2 teaspoons grated fresh ginger
Pinch ground allspice
Pinch ground cinnamon
Pinch ground cumin
Pinch ground cloves

1. In a small saucepan, gently heat together the butter and maple syrup until the butter melts.
2. Remove from the heat and stir in the ginger, allspice, cinnamon, cumin, and cloves. Use the glaze right away.

Makes about ½ cup

∽

COOL CARDAMOM DRESSING

1 cup buttermilk
Pinch ground cardamom
1 clove garlic, crushed and minced
Salt and freshly ground black
   pepper to taste

Mix all ingredients in a small bowl.

Makes about 1 cup

∽

Mango Soup

I love mangoes, so I swirl up this soup by the buckets when they're in season.

1 cup fresh orange juice
¼ cup dried apricots
2 large ripe mangoes, peeled and sliced
2 teaspoons fresh lime juice
1 cup plain yogurt or sour cream

1. In a medium saucepan, combine the orange juice and apricots, cover, and gently simmer until the apricots soften, about 20 minutes.

2. Place the mangoes and the lime juice in a blender or food processor, and puree. Add the orange juice and apricots, and puree again.

3. Pour the mixture into a glass or earthenware bowl, and let it cool to room temperature. Stir in the yogurt or sour cream. Cover and frigerate until thoroughly chilled.

Serves 4 to 6

Raclette

This superb dish of potatoes and cheese is most satisfying on those blustery nights when summer is giving way to fall. The salad's piquant seasoning contrasts nicely with the rich flavors of the main course.

Special Equipment: Wooden skewers soaked in water for 30 minutes before grilling

Grill Temperature: High

8 new potatoes

6 boiling onions

Marinade:

½ cup dry white wine

2 tablespoons extra virgin olive oil

1 clove garlic, crushed and minced

2 tablespoons grated or finely minced white onion

2 tablespoons minced fresh tarragon or thyme, or 1 tablespoon crumbled dried tarragon or thyme

Pinch salt

Freshly ground black pepper to taste

16 ounces raclette, Gruyère, or Jarlsberg cheese, cut into cubes

Crusty French bread

Mustard Sauce (page 79)

1. Blanch the potatoes in boiling water until you can just pierce them with a knife, about 6 to 8 minutes, or blanch them in the microwave.

2. Blanch the onions in boiling water until soft, but not mushy, about 5 minutes, or blanch them in the microwave.

3. In a bowl or baking dish, combine the wine, olive oil, garlic, grated or minced onion, tarragon or thyme, salt, and pepper. Cut the potatoes in half and add them to the wine mixture. Toss well, cover, and refrigerate for 3 hours or more.

4. Thread the potatoes onto the skewers, alternating the onions and the cheese. Pour the marinade through a strainer or fine sieve, and reserve for the Mustard Sauce.

5. Brush the grill with vegetable oil. Place the skewers on the grill, and cook, turning often, until the cheese becomes gooey and the potatoes char lightly, 4 to 6 minutes.

6. Serve immediately, with French bread and Mustard Sauce.

Serves 4 to 5

MUSTARD SAUCE

2 tablespoons unsalted butter

2 tablespoons unbleached flour

1 cup warm milk

1 tablespoon Dijon mustard

*3 tablespoons strained Raclette
marinade (page 78)*

*Salt and freshly ground black
pepper to taste*

1. In a wide saucepan, melt the butter. Stir in the flour and cook, stirring constantly, over low heat, for about 3 minutes, until you have a faintly golden paste.

2. Pour in the milk, switch to a wire whisk, and continue to stir until the mixture thickens. Add the mustard and strained marinade, and cook, still stirring, until thick and smooth, about 5 minutes.

3. Season with salt and pepper.

Makes about 1 cup

∾

ZINGY ORANGY TOMATOES

*½ teaspoon finely grated orange
zest*

¼ cup fresh orange juice

2 teaspoons extra virgin olive oil

*2 teaspoons finely minced fresh
oregano*

*2 teaspoons finely minced fresh
basil*

*2 ripe Roma tomatoes, cut into
chunks*

In a glass or ceramic bowl, combine the ingredients. Toss well and serve.

Serves 4

79
∾

Satay Skewers

A hearty dish for appetites immune to the sun, tempered by a light and zesty soup.

Special Equipment: Wooden skewers soaked in water for 30 minutes before grilling

Grill Temperature: High

1 *14-ounce container extra-firm tofu*

8 cherry tomatoes

16 large firm white mushrooms, washed and trimmed, halved or quartered, depending on size

Peanut Sauce (right), 1 recipe

1 cup raw couscous, cooked according to package directions

1. Press the tofu: Place a few layers of paper towels on a table or counter, and put the tofu on them. Cover the tofu with a few more layer of towels, then lay a cutting board over that, with a heavy skillet on top. Let it rest until the water's been squeezed out, about an hour, then cut the tofu into cubes.

2. Toss the tofu, tomatoes, and mushrooms with the Peanut Sauce to coat them well.

3. Thread them onto separate skewers, and grill until the tomatoes start to char, 6 to 8 minutes, the tofu turns a golden brown, 8 to 12 minutes, and the mushrooms are cooked through, 12 minutes or more.

4. Prepare couscous.

5. Remove vegetables from skewers and serve immediately over couscous.

Serves 4 to 6

Peanut Sauce

¼ cup crunchy peanut butter

1 cup warm water

2 teaspoons soy sauce

2 tablespoons fresh orange juice

½ teaspoon ground coriander

½ teaspoon ground cumin

1 teaspoon grated fresh ginger

1 clove garlic, grated

½ teaspoon cayenne pepper (or, to taste)

1. Whisk together the peanut butter and water until smooth.

2. Whisk in the remaining ingredients, until well blended.

Makes about 1¼ cups

Strawberry Soup

4 dried apricots

16 ounces apple juice, unfiltered or regular

1 pint strawberries, washed and hulled

½ cup buttermilk

1 tablespoon fresh lemon juice

Sliced strawberries

1 tablespoon grated lemon zest

1. Soak the apricots in apple juice for at least 3 hours, or overnight in the refrigerator, until softened. Transfer to a nonreactive medium saucepan (enamel or any pan that is not aluminum) and simmer gently until the apricots turn mushy and the juice thickens, about 10 minutes.

2. Puree the pint of strawberries in a blender or food processor. Add the juice-and-apricot mixture and blend until smooth. Add buttermilk and blend again. Chill for at least 3 hours.

3. Just before serving, stir in the lemon juice. Garnish with additional sliced strawberries and a sprinkle of lemon zest.

Serves 4 to 6

SESAME SHIITAKE MUSHROOMS

These mushrooms are sweet and smoky, and at their best when bathed in their own marinade and served over zesty Pepper-Flecked Rice.

SPECIAL EQUIPMENT: Wooden skewers soaked in water 30 minutes before grilling

GRILL TEMPERATURE: High (use honey wood chips for added flavor if available)

Marinade:
¹/₄ cup dry sherry

¹/₄ cup pineapple juice

2 tablespoons soy sauce

1 clove garlic, crushed and minced

1 1-inch piece fresh ginger, peeled and grated

¹/₂ cup hoisin sauce

12 shiitake mushrooms, fresh or dried, reconstituted according to package directions

1 14-ounce container extra-firm tofu, cut into 1-inch cubes

2 firm slender Japanese eggplant, ends trimmed, cut into 1-inch segments

1 cup fresh pineapple chunks or pineapple chunks canned in juice, drained

1 cup (approximately) sesame seeds

1. To make the marinade, in a glass or ceramic bowl or baking dish, combine the ingredients for the marinade. Stir well to blend.

2. To prepare the mushrooms, place the mushrooms, tofu, eggplant, and pineapple in the marinade. Stir well to coat. Cover and refrigerate for at least 3 hours and up to 18 hours.

3. Remove the vegetables from the marinade and thread them onto the skewers, alternating mushrooms, tofu cubes, eggplant, and pineapple chunks until you've used them up. They should fill 4 medium skewers. Reserve the remaining marinade.

4. Spread the sesame seeds on a cookie sheet. Roll the skewers over the seeds, to coat.

5. Grill the skewers, turning often, until

the seeds have blackened and the mushrooms are cooked through, about 10 minutes.

6. Transfer the remaining marinade to a heatproof dish and place over the hot grill. Cover with foil and let boil until it reduces and thickens, about 5 minutes.

7. Serve the skewers immediately over rice, drizzled with the reserved marinade.

Serves 4 to 6

PEPPER-FLECKED RICE

1 cup raw short-grain brown or white rice

1 yellow bell pepper, grilled, and diced (pages 34-35)

1 red bell pepper, grilled, and diced (pages 34-35)

½ cup canned water chestnuts, diced

1. Prepare the rice according to the package directions.

2. Transfer the cooked rice to a large mixing bowl, and let it cool to room temperature. Add the diced peppers and the water chestnuts, and toss well.

Serves 4 to 6

CHAPTER 5

Diverse Hearty Dishes:
Filled Vegetables, Grilled Grains,
and More . . .

∾

FILLED GRILLED TOMATOES

ROASTED VIDALIA ONIONS

STUFFED MUSHROOMS

GRILLED BABA GANOUSH

GRILLED MUSHROOMS ON TOAST

CHEESE TOASTED TOMATO SLICES

SMOKY AND SPICY BROCCOLI AND
BEAN CURD

GRILLED CHEESE GRITS

POLENTA

FOCACCIA

FILLED GRILLED TOMATOES

Here's how to celebrate a surfeit of plump, ripe tomatoes.

GRILL TEMPERATURE: Medium

⅓ cup extra virgin olive oil

Juice of ½ lemon

1 teaspoon crumbled dried thyme

Pinch salt

Freshly ground black pepper to taste

4 large ripe but firm tomatoes

Cream Pesto (right)

Grated imported Parmesan or Asiago cheese to taste

1. Combine the olive oil, lemon juice, thyme, salt, pepper, and stir well.
2. Slice off the stem end and opposite end of each tomato, then cut each tomato in half horizontally.
3. With a teaspoon scoop out the seeds, making a small well in each half.
4. Brush the grill and tomatoes with the lemon-thyme oil, and grill, well side down, until the tomatoes soften. Transfer them to a plate, turn them over, and fill each well with pesto. Sprinkle the pesto with cheese.
5. Return the tomatoes to the grill, well side up. Cover loosely with foil, and grill until the cheese turns golden.

Serves 4

CREAM PESTO

½ cup Crème Fraîche (page 95)

1 clove garlic, crushed and minced

½ cup grated imported Parmesan cheese

½ cup minced fresh basil

With a mortar and pestle, a blender, or a food processor, combine all the ingredients until thoroughly blended.

Makes about 1½ cups

Cucumber Dill Soup

A revivifying soup I drink with abandon when the mercury rises unmercifully.

1 clove garlic, crushed and minced
2 cups plain yogurt
*2 firm cucumbers, peeled and
    finely minced*
*¼ cup minced fresh dill (or more,
    to taste)*
½ teaspoon paprika
Salt to taste

1. In a mixing bowl, combine the garlic and yogurt, and beat with a whisk until the yogurt is smooth and light.
2. Whisk in the cucumbers, dill, paprika, and salt.
3. Refrigerate until well chilled, at least 3 hours. Keeps, covered and refrigerated, up to 4 days.

Serves 4

Roasted Vidalia Onions

Here's a treat you shouldn't pass up : an incomparable concoction comprising mild Vidalia onions filled with pureed fruit and nuts.

GRILL TEMPERATURE: High

4 Vidalia onions
2 cups Fruit and Nut Paste (right)
¼ cup (approximately) unsalted butter, melted

1. Boil the onions in about 4 inches of water, until just soft, or soften in the microwave. Carve off the top. Remove the core and discard it. Carefully lift out enough of the inner layers to leave a wall about ⅛ inch thick. Divide paste into 4 equal portions.

2. For each onion: Spread the cavity with a thin film of paste. Carefully replace a single layer of the onion. Spread this layer with paste, then replace the next layer. Continue until you've used up the paste, discarding what remains of the onion or saving it for another use.

3. Brush each onion with the butter, place it on the grill, and cover with the grill lid or with aluminum foil. Grill, turning over after 6 minutes, until the onion and the filling virtually melt together, about 10 to 15 minutes.

Serves 4

FRUIT AND NUT PASTE

1½ cups pitted prunes
½ cup ground walnuts

1. Place the prunes in a medium saucepan, and cover with water.

2. Bring to a boil and simmer, covered, until prunes are plump and soft, about 20 minutes.

3. Drain them well and transfer them to a blender or food processor. Process into a thick paste, taking care not to liquefy. Add the walnuts and process again briefly until well blended.

Makes about 2 cups

GRILLED EGGPLANT RELISH

This incomparable condiment is addictive. Try it on Vidalia onions and grilled dishes of all kinds and on buttered, lightly grilled bread.

2 Japanese eggplant, sliced in half lengthwise

1 red bell pepper, halved, cored, and seeded

1 tablespoon extra virgin olive oil

1 tablespoon fresh lemon juice

1 teaspoon red pepper sauce (such as Tabasco)

3 tablespoons finely chopped onion

2 cloves garlic, crushed and minced

Pinch sugar

Salt to taste

1. Brush the grill with vegetable oil and place the eggplant and pepper on it. Grill until their skins char. Transfer the pepper to a paper bag, and turn over the eggplant to grill the other side.

2. When the eggplant is soft throughout, take it off the grill and set it aside until it's cool enough to handle.

3. Peel off the pepper skin and slice the pepper thinly. Scoop out the eggplant pulp and chop.

4. In a mixing bowl, combine the eggplant, roasted pepper, olive oil, lemon juice, red pepper sauce, onion, garlic, and sugar. Season with salt.

Makes about 2 cups

QUICK CURRIED COOLER

This soup is a bracing tonic: fast, refreshing, delicious.

1 cup plain yogurt
1 tablespoon fresh lemon juice
1 tablespoon curry powder
1 teaspoon ground cumin
3 cups tomato juice
2 large cucumbers, peeled and chopped
¼ cup minced fresh parsley
Salt and freshly ground black pepper
    to taste

1. In a large glass or earthenware bowl, whisk the yogurt until it's light and smooth.
2. Whisk in the lemon juice, curry powder, and cumin.
3. Add the tomato juice, and stir until well blended. Add the cucumbers, parsley, and salt and pepper.
4. Cover with plastic wrap and refrigerate until chilled through, at least 3 hours.

Serves 6

❧

STUFFED MUSHROOMS

This excellent dish is known as a "cheat," hinging not on your skill, but on the quality of your ingredients. Good cheese and good, firm mushrooms guarantee good results.

SPECIAL EQUIPMENT: Fine-mesh grate

GRILL TEMPERATURE: Medium

12 large firm white mushrooms, washed
and trimmed (cavities measuring
roughly 1½ inches in diameter)

¼ to ⅓ cup extra virgin olive oil

Filling:
1 cup Boursin cheese with garlic and
herbs, or 1 cup Cream Pesto (page 86),
or ½ cup ricotta cheese blended with
¼ cup grated imported Parmesan cheese
and ¼ cup finely shredded mozzarella
cheese

1. Clean the mushrooms and remove the stems.
2. Brush the grill and the mushrooms with olive oil, and place the mushrooms on the grill, stem side down, until lightly browned at the edges.
3. Remove the mushrooms and fill the cavities with Boursin, Cream Pesto, or ricotta, Parmesan, and mozzarella.
4. Return the mushrooms to the grill, filling side up, and cover loosely with foil. Grill until the filling is bubbling away. Serve immediately.

Serves 4 to 6

91
∾

Succotash Salad

The word *succotash* was used among different Native American tribes to denote a stew composed of everything on hand, which nearly always included corn. You can take a lot of liberties with succotash, since it's a free-form dish from the start. Here's the version I like best.

1 tablespoon unsalted butter

1 small red onion, chopped

2 cups cooked black beans

2 cups cooked fresh corn kernels

1/3 cup corn oil (unrefined, if available)

1 tablespoon fresh lime juice

1 tablespoon red wine vinegar

1 clove garlic, crushed and minced

1 tablespoon green* or red salsa

1 tablespoon ground cumin

Pinch cayenne pepper

Salt to taste

1. In a skillet, melt the butter and sauté the onion until soft. Add the black beans and corn, and stir well to combine. Remove from the heat and transfer to a large mixing bowl.
2. Mix together all of the remaining ingredients and toss with the bean mixture. Serve chilled or at room temperature.

Serves 4 to 6

*See appendix for mail-order sources.

Grilled Baba Ganoush

Baba ganoush, a seasoned eggplant dish, is not only better but easier when made on the grill. Aside from mixing the tahini sauce, there's nothing to do in advance—just light the coals and proceed.

SPECIAL EQUIPMENT: Fine-mesh grate

GRILL TEMPERATURE: High

4 slender Japanese eggplant

¼ cup toasted or regular tahini*

1 tablespoon hot water

2 tablespoons plain yogurt

1 clove garlic, grated

2 tablespoons finely minced fresh cilantro

1 tablespoon fresh lemon juice

1 teaspoon ground cumin

1 teaspoon paprika

2 tablespoons lightly toasted sesame seeds (page 27)

Pinch of salt

1. Pierce each eggplant in several places with a knife. Place the eggplant, whole, on the grill, and grill, turning often, until the skin has buckled and charred evenly.

2. Take the eggplant off the grill and set aside to cool.

3. Meanwhile, make the sauce by whisking together the tahini and hot water until smooth. Whisk in the yogurt, garlic, cilantro, lemon juice, cumin, paprika, sesame seeds, and salt.

4. When the eggplant are cool enough to handle, slice each in half lengthwise, as if it were a baked potato. Spoon an equal portion of tahini sauce into each, mash it into the pulp, and serve.

Serves 4

*See appendix for mail-order sources.

93

FRUITY TABBOULEH

Fresh fruits temper the hearty grain in this dish, which is satisfying yet light, in short, just right for a hot summer night.

1 cup water

1 cup fine bulgur wheat

1/3 cup toasted slivered almonds (page 74)

1/3 cup raisins

2 tablespoons finely shredded unsweetened coconut (optional)

1 cup chopped fresh fruit (such as grapes, pineapple, peaches, strawberries, blueberries)

1 cup plain yogurt

1. Bring the water to a boil in a medium saucepan.
2. Sprinkle in the bulgur wheat, cover, and remove from the heat. Let the wheat absorb the water for 40 minutes.
3. Transfer to a large mixing bowl and add almonds, raisins, coconut, if desired, fresh fruit, and yogurt.
4. Refrigerate until well chilled.

Serves 6 to 8

❧

Grilled Mushrooms on Toast

Here's one of my favorite swift suppers, a down-home version of a popular Parisian dish. Look for crème fraîche in the cheese section of your supermarket or in a cheese specialty shop. Or make your own a night or more ahead of time.

SPECIAL EQUIPMENT: Fine-mesh grate

GRILL TEMPERATURE: High (use honey wood chips for additional flavor if available)

4 tablespoons (¼ cup) unsalted butter

1 small clove garlic, crushed and minced

1 shallot, minced

2 tablespoons minced fresh chives

1 pound wood ear or oyster mushrooms, cleaned and dried

4 tablespoons Crème Fraîche (right)

4 tablespoons comte cheese (a soft, mild cheese)

4 slices French bread, lightly toasted (on the grill, if you wish)

1. In a small saucepan, melt the butter. Stir in the garlic, shallot, and chives.
2. With a soft pastry brush, slather the butter onto the mushrooms. Place the mushrooms on the fine-mesh grate and grill, turning occasionally, until the mushrooms are cooked through and a crust starts to form, about 8 minutes.
3. In a large mixing bowl, toss the mushrooms with the Crème Fraîche until well coated, then toss again with the *comte* cheese.
4. Distribute the mixture evenly among the pieces of toast. Serve immediately.

Serves 2

CRÈME FRAÎCHE

1 cup heavy cream, at room temperature

⅓ cup buttermilk, at room temperature

1. In a glass or earthenware bowl, combine the heavy cream and buttermilk. Cover with plastic wrap and let sit at room temperature for 12 hours, until thickened.
2. Transfer to a glass or plastic container with a tight-fitting lid. It will keep, refrigerated, for up to 5 days.

Makes about 1 cup

RED CABBAGE AND FRESH BERRIES

It's too bad that cabbage, which ought to be prized for its sweet, subtle flavor, is so often shunned because of its unpleasant aroma. This tasty dish exploits its affinity for fresh summer fruits.

2 tablespoons unsalted butter
1 cup chopped red onion
1 small clove garlic, minced
2 tablespoons minced fresh parsley
4 cups shredded red cabbage
¼ cup red wine
1 teaspoon grated orange zest
Pinch salt
½ cup fresh blueberries
½ cup washed, hulled, and sliced fresh strawberries
¼ cup dried cranberries* (optional)

1. In a large skillet, melt the butter. Sauté the onion, garlic, and parsley until the onion softens and becomes translucent, about 6 to 8 minutes.

2. Add the cabbage, wine, orange zest, and salt, and cook over low heat, stirring occasionally, until the cabbage wilts, about 20 minutes.

3. Remove from the heat and transfer to a large mixing bowl. While the mixture is still warm, toss in the blueberries, strawberries, and dried cranberries, if desired. Mix well and serve warm or at room temperature.

Serves 6

*SEE APPENDIX FOR MAIL-ORDER SOURCES.

CHEESE TOASTED TOMATO SLICES

Simple, satisfying, and delicious, these crispy tomato slices are addictive. The soup is the summer house specialty at my favorite Middle Eastern restaurant, Saam, in Pasadena, California.

GRILL TEMPERATURE: High

½ cup unbleached flour

⅓ cup yellow cornmeal

⅓ cup grated imported Parmesan cheese

2 tablespoons minced fresh oregano or 1 tablespoon crumbled dried oregano

2 eggs, lightly beaten

Salt and freshly ground black pepper to taste

4 medium firm tomatoes, sliced into ¼-inch-thick rounds

1. In a wide bowl, combine the flour, cornmeal, cheese, oregano, eggs, and salt and pepper to taste. Dredge the tomato slices in the mixture, coating each side.

2. Brush the grill with vegetable oil, and spread the slices on top. Grill the slices, turning once, until they're golden crisp, about 8 to 10 minutes.

Serves 6 to 8

TANGY SPINACH SOUP

2 to 3 tablespoons extra virgin olive oil

1 large leek, white part only, chopped

1 large white onion, chopped

2 cloves garlic, crushed and minced

1 cup minced fresh parsley

1 cup minced fresh cilantro

½ cup minced fresh mint

2 cups fresh spinach, coarsely chopped

3 cups plain yogurt

6 cups water

1 cup cooked rice

1. In a large saucepan, heat the olive oil. Sauté the leek, onion, and garlic until soft and translucent, about 8 minutes.

2. Add the parsley, cilantro, mint, and spinach, and continue to cook, stirring often, over low heat until the spinach has wilted, about 4 minutes.

3. Meanwhile, whip the yogurt with a whisk until it's light and smooth. Stir in the water, and add to the saucepan. Heat gently, and stir in the rice, taking care not to boil.

Serves 8

Smoky and Spicy Broccoli and Bean Curd

Bean curd (tofu) takes on the flavor of anything used to season it, in this case a ginger-infused soy sauce, which grilling sets off to excellent effect.

SPECIAL EQUIPMENT: Fine-mesh grate

GRILL TEMPERATURE: High

2 tablespoons brown-rice vinegar

3 tablespoons soy sauce

1 tablespoon honey

2 tablespoons sherry

1 teaspoon ground mustard

Red pepper flakes to taste

1 tablespoon cornstarch or arrowroot

2 tablespoons grated fresh ginger

2 cloves garlic, crushed and minced

¼ cup finely minced scallions, white part only

¾ cup water

1 pound broccoli, tough outer stalks trimmed and pared, blanched

1 14-ounce container extra-firm tofu, pressed (Satay Skewers, page 80, step 1) and sliced ½ inch thick

1 cup raw white rice, cooked according to package directions

1. In a saucepan, combine the vinegar, soy sauce, honey, sherry, mustard, red pepper flakes, cornstarch or arrowroot, ginger, garlic, scallions, and water. Bring the mixture to a simmer and cook, stirring constantly, until it thickens, about 7 minutes.

2. Brush the mixture onto the broccoli and tofu, and grill until the tofu is warmed through and the broccoli is tender, about 6 to 8 minutes.

3. Drizzle the broccoli and tofu with the remaining sauce, and serve over rice at once.

Serve 4 to 6

PEACH SOUP

This sweet and creamy soup may make dessert redundant.

4 dried peaches
2 cups fresh orange juice
1 dried or fresh bay leaf
4 to 6 medium very ripe fresh peaches
½ cup milk (part skim, if you'd like)
⅓ cup plain yogurt, sour cream, or soy substitute
Pinch ground nutmeg
Pinch ground ginger

1. Soak the dried peaches in the orange juice for at least 3 hours or overnight, until softened. Transfer the mixture to a nonreactive saucepan (enamel or any pan that is not aluminum) and add the bay leaf. Simmer gently until the dried peaches begin to disintegrate and turn mushy, about 10 minutes.

2. Bring a large pot of water to a boil. Plunge in the fresh peaches for about 15 seconds, until the skins slip off easily. Skin and pit the peaches, transfer to a food processor or blender, and puree.

3. Remove the bay leaf from the orange juice mixture, and add the mixture to the peach puree. Blend until smooth. Add the milk and blend again.

4. Chill at least 3 hours. Just before serving, stir in the yogurt, sour cream, or soy substitute. Add the nutmeg and ginger and stir.

Serves 4 to 6

Grilled Cheese Grits

Despite the rigorous efforts of several notable Southern chefs, grits haven't caught on in the rest of the country, where they figure more commonly in jokes than meal planning. But pummeled with good sharp cheddar, seasoned with piquant garlic and herbs, and grilled until golden brown, they deserve serious consideration.

Grill Temperature: Medium

4 cups lightly salted water

1 cup white grits (not quick-cooking or instant)

1 cup shredded sharp cheddar cheese

2 tablespoons unsalted butter

Minced jalapeño peppers (optional)

Salt to taste

2 to 4 tablespoons butter, melted

1 clove garlic, minced

Minced fresh herb of your choice: cilantro, mint, oregano, chives

1. Bring the water to a boil and slowly stir in the grits.

2. Reduce the heat, and simmer, stirring often, until the grits are creamy and smooth, about 40 minutes.

3. Remove the grits from the heat, and stir in the cheese and 2 tablespoons of butter. Add the jalapeños as well, if you'd like. Season with salt.

4. Pour the grits into a pie plate, and let cool. Refrigerate until firm, about 3 hours.

5. Slice the grits into wedges about 1/2 inch thick. Combine the melted butter, garlic, and herb. Brush the grits with the garlic-and-herb butter.

6. Brush the grill with vegetable oil to prevent sticking. Grill the wedges until they begin to brown, about 4 to 6 minutes on each side.

Serves 6 to 8

The Perfect Lemonade

Lemonade can be crisp and revivifying, or it can be as dull as an August afternoon, watery and oversweet. The "perfect" lemonade is a highly personal business, hitting the palate directly in the realm where it's most sensitive and particular: sweet-and-sour. Consequently, there's only one way to serve perfect lemonade, and that's to let your guests mix their own.

1 lemon

1 chilled tall glass or tumbler

Superfine granulated sugar to taste

⅔ cup water, chilled (sparkling mineral water, if desired)

Ice cubes to taste

1. Squeeze the juice from the lemon and transfer it into the chilled glass.
2. Add sugar and stir until it dissolves.
3. Stir in the water and the ice. Adjust sweetening to taste.

Serves 1

❧

POLENTA

Grilling turns drab cornmeal mush into an alluring treat: soft, savory squares with a golden crisp crust.

GRILL TEMPERATURE: Medium

3 cups lightly salted water

¾ cup coarse yellow cornmeal

One or more of the following (optional): grated cheese (such as imported Parmesan, fontina, or Asiago or sharp cheddar or Monterey Jack), chopped sun-dried tomatoes, fresh corn kernels, roasted chili peppers, poblano or jalapeño (page 35), grated onion

4 tablespoons butter, melted

1 clove garlic, minced

Minced fresh herb of your choice: basil, oregano, rosemary

Topping:
  One or more of the following (optional): tomatoes, grilled (page 41); fennel, grilled (page 31); red peppers, grilled (pages 34-35); onions, grilled (page 34); garlic, grilled (page 32); eggplant, grilled (page 30)

1. In a large saucepan, bring the water to a boil.

2. Sprinkle the cornmeal in an even flow into the water, rather than pouring it in all at once. Stir and simmer, continuing to stir until the mixture is thick enough to pull away from the pot and stand on its own, about 30 to 40 minutes. Quickly add the optional ingredients of your choice, if desired. Stir well, and remove polenta from the heat.

3. Pour the polenta into a pie plate, and let it cool. Refrigerate until firm, about 3 hours.

4. Slice the polenta into wedges about ½ inch thick. Combine the melted butter, garlic, and herb. Brush the polenta with the garlic-and-herb butter.

5. Brush the grill with vegetable oil to prevent sticking. Grill the wedges until they begin to brown, about 4 to 6 minutes on each side.

6. Serve topped with the grilled vegetables or vegetable combination of your choice.

Serves 6

FOCACCIA

A versatile showcase for grilled vegetables of all kinds. *Focaccia* makes optimum use of heat and time. You can cook a variety of vegetables for the topping while the coals are very hot, then finish the *focaccia* once the fire's cooled down.

SPECIAL EQUIPMENT: Fine-mesh grate

GRILL TEMPERATURE: High for grilling the toppings; medium for the *focaccia*

Topping:
 One or more of the following (optional): onions, grilled (page 34); fresh tomatoes, grilled (page 41), or sun-dried tomatoes, reconstituted according to package directions, or a combination of the two; mushrooms, grilled (page 33); bell peppers, grilled (pages 34-35); eggplant, grilled (page 30)

Herb-Flavored Oil of your choice (page 105)

1 fully baked 8-inch focaccia or pizza shell

Grated imported Parmesan, fontina, or Asiago cheese or shredded mozzarella, provolone, or Monterey Jack cheese to taste

1. If you're going to be grilling vegetables for the topping, proceed according to the recipe of your choice.

2. Once you've prepared the topping, let the coals cool down to a medium temperature. Fit the grill with the fine-mesh grate.

3. Stir the Herb-Flavored Oil well and brush it onto the *focaccia*. Distribute the grilled vegetables evenly on top. Sprinkle with cheese.

4. Place the *focaccia* on the grate, and cover the grill loosely with foil.

5. Grill, checking often, until the cheese melts or until the *focaccia* is heated through. The timing will vary widely, between 4 to 10 minutes or more, depending on the thickness of the crust and the temperature of the coals.

Serves 4

*FOCACCIA IS AVAILABLE IN MOST SUPER-MARKETS. CHECK THE BREAD SECTION OR THE SPECIALTY FOODS SECTION. SEE APPENDIX FOR MAIL-ORDER SOURCES.

Herb-Flavored Oil

¼ cup extra virgin olive oil
¼ cup fresh rosemary
Pinch coarse salt

Combine the ingredients and stir well before using.

Makes about ½ cup

❧

Variation with Basil and Oregano: Substitute 2 tablespoons minced fresh basil and 2 tablespoons minced fresh oregano for the rosemary and salt.

105
❧

APPENDIX

It's so easy to find good prepared condiments, such as chutneys, flavored vinegars, marinades, mustards, and relishes of all kinds that it's possible to skip the time-consuming steps involved in preparing your own. What's more, thanks to these diverse, virtually ubiquitous products, you can modify and diversify basic recipes without end; a new marinade renders a new dish.

You don't have to go out of your way to get some of the best of these prepared foods. In fact, you don't have to go anywhere at all. Here is a select list of mail-order companies that will take orders by phone or fax and deliver the goods promptly.

106

AMERICAN SPOON FOODS
P.O. Box 566
1668 Clarion Avenue
Petosky, MI 49770
(800) 222-5886
(616) 347-9030
FAX: (616) 347-2512

All other contenders duly considered, I've concluded that the sincerest form of flattery is lugging twelve 10-ounce jars of fruit conserves halfway around the world. American Spoon Foods' products are so good, I brought them as gifts when I traveled from Boston to Tuscany, to meet my new in-laws.

Besides conserves and preserves, American Spoon Foods makes salsas, chutneys, marinades, and barbecue sauces, all of which are no less flavorful for being fat-free.

CHUKAR CHERRIES
306 Wine Country Road
Prosser, WA 99350-0510
(800) 624-9544
(509) 786-2055

Those who love cherries need no longer lament that their favorite fruit is so briefly in season. Pam and Guy Auld have found a way to preserve cherries perfectly. They dry them, rendering deep red "raisins" that taste intensely like the fruit. In addition to dried cherries, they make marinades, barbecue sauces, salad dressings, chutneys, and baking mixes containing them.

HAMMACHER SCHLEMMER
(800) 543-3366

HARRY AND DAVID
Call for the latest catalogue: (800) 345-5655

The folks best known for the Fruit-of-the-Month Club also offer a number of barbecue kits, packed with marinades and barbecue sauces and wood chips in a number of flavors.

MEADOWBROOK HERB CATALOGUE
93 Kingstown Road
Wyoming, RI 02898
(401) 539-0209

Meadowbrook is a dependable source for dried herbs, reliable for both prompt delivery and consistent quality. Organically grown, their dried herbs taste fresher than any I've tried. They also have special barbecue blends.

WALNUT ACRES ORGANIC FARMS
Walnut Acres Road
Penns Creek, PA 17862
(800) 433-3998
(717) 837-0601
FAX: (717) 837-1146

The supermarket of natural food mail-order firms, Walnut Acres, I've found always delivers on the considerable promise held out by its enticing, encyclopedic catalogue. In addition to prepared foods such as dressings, marinades, and sugar-free catsup, Walnut Acres will send organic produce, dairy products, herbs, and spices.

There are two terrific catalogues to consult for more mail-order merchants: Jeanne Heifetz's conscientiously researched, aptly detailed *Green Groceries: A Mail Order Guide to Organic Foods by Mail* (HarperPerennial) and *Food Finds,* Allison and Margaret Engels' enthusiastic, anecdotal guide to "America's Best Local Foods and the People Who Produce Them" (HarperPerennial).

107

INDEX

~

111

CONVERSION CHART
Equivalent Imperial and Metric Measurements

American cooks use standard containers, the 8-ounce cup and a tablespoon that takes exactly 16 level fillings to fill that cup level. Measuring by cup makes it very difficult to give weight equivalents, as a cup of densely packed butter will weigh considerably more than a cup of flour. The easiest way therefore to deal with cup measurements in recipes is to take the amount by volume rather than by weight. Thus the equation reads:

$$1 \text{ cup} = 240 \text{ ml} = 8 \text{ fl. oz.} \qquad \frac{1}{2} \text{ cup} = 120 \text{ ml} = 4 \text{ fl. oz.}$$

It is possible to buy a set of American cup measures in major stores around the world. In the States, butter is often measured in sticks. One stick is the equivalent of 8 tablespoons. One tablespoon of butter is therefore the equivalent to 1/2 ounce /15 grams.

Liquid Measures

Fluid ounces	U.S.	Imperial	Milliliters
	1 teaspoon	1 teaspoon	5
1/4	2 teaspoons	1 dessertspoon	7
1/2	1 tablespoon	1 tablespoon	15
1	2 tablespoons	2 tablespoons	28
2	1/4 cup	4 tablespoons	56
	1/2 cup or 1/4 pint		110
		1/4 pint or 1 gill	140
	3/4 cup		170
	1 cup or 1/2 pint		225
9			250, 1/4 liter
10	1 1/4 cups	1/2 pint	280
12	1 1/2 cups	3/4 pint	340
15		3/4 pint	420
16	2 cups or 1 pint		450
18	2 1/4 cups		500, 1/2 liter
20	2 1/2 cups	1 pint	560
24	3 cups or 1 1/2 pints		675
25		1 1/4 pints	700
27	3 1/2 cups		750
30	3 3/4 cups	1 1/2 pints	840
32	4 cups or 2 pints or 1 quart	900	
35		1 3/4 pints	980
36	4 1/2 cups		1000, 1 liter
40	5 cups or 2 1/2 pints	2 pints or 1 quart	1120
48	6 cups or 3 pints		1350

Solid Measures

U.S. and Imperial Measures		Metric Measures	
Ounces	Pounds	Grams	Kilos
1		28	
2		56	
3	1/2	100	
4	1/4	112	
5		140	
6		168	
8	1/2	225	
9		250	1/4
12	3/4	340	
16	1	450	
18		500	1/2
20	1 1/4	560	
24	1 1/2	675	
27		750	3/4
28	1 3/4	780	
32	2	900	
36	2 1/4	1000	1
40	2 1/2	1100	
48	3	1350	
54		1500	1 1/2
64	4	1800	
72	4 1/2	2000	2
80	5	2250	2 1/4
90		2500	2 1/2
100	6	2800	2 3/4

Oven Temperature Equivalents

Fahrenheit	Celsius	Gas Mark	Description
225	110	1/4	Cool
250	130	1/2	
275	140	1	Very Slow
300	150	2	
325	170	3	Slow
350	180	4	Moderate
375	190	5	
400	200	6	Moderately Hot
425	220	7	Fairly Hot
450	230	8	Hot
475	240	9	Very Hot
500	250	10	Extremely Hot

Linear and Area Measures

1 inch	2.54 centimeters
1 foot	0.3048 meters
1 square inch	6.4516 square centimeters
1 square foot	929.03 square centimeters